TROTSKY
The Great Debate Renewed

TROTSKY

The Great Debate Renewed

Editor

NICOLAS KRASSÓ

London University

Introduction by David Horowitz

ST. LOUIS, MISSOURI | NEW CRITICS PRESS, INC. | 1972

Published simultaneously in Canada
by Clarke, Irwin & Company Limited, Toronto and Vancouver

Library of Congress Catalog Card Number: 70–146986

SBN 0–87853–002–9

Introduction

One important lesson that the American New Left has learned to its cost over the last decade has been the wisdom of Lenin's dictum, that "without revolutionary theory, there can be no revolutionary movement." During its brief existence as a political presence, the New Left witnessed the release of vast political energies of change, and itself led massive political protests against the war in Vietnam. At the same time, however, it was unable to create a viable political instrument of its own, or to develop and sustain itself as a coherent political movement. Running the gamut from an initially "anti-ideological" posture to a feverish embrace of sectarian Marxisms and anarchism, the New Left entered the 1970's as a tendency without organization, a movement without direction—or, rather, with such a diversity of directions as to constitute a mere drift in the social and political currents of the time, rather than a driving force of revolutionary change.

In both its initial desire not to be continuous with any past or tradition, to create itself *ex nihil*—and in its sudden impulsive adoption of prefabricated ideological constructs and political identities, the New Left revealed its peculiarly American roots. For America is itself the "new nation," willfully created: a unique rupture in the historical process. It is a land without a visible past, or more accurately, where the past is constantly being erased by the technologies of commerce, and the markets cult of the disposable, the obsolescent, and the new. To invent theory as one goes along, to conjure identities at will (and abandon them when they prove inadequate) is wholly American, and in the true tradition of its pragmatic gospel. Likewise the search for ready-made replacements for worn-out theories, the expedient appropriation of ideologies that have worked for others.

But have they? And if so, to what extent? Under what conditions? And in what context?

To revolutionize a social order, it is as necessary to understand the process of revolution as it is to understand the structure of the *status quo*. The revolutionary movement, no less than the social order which it seeks to change, *is* what it has been; and what it is, moreover, sets the limits of what it can become. A revolutionary theory that does not understand the conditions of revolutionary success—not only the errors of failed revolutions, but the failure of successful revolutions—does not begin to be adequate to the task at hand.

At the gateway to any attempt to establish a critical understanding of modern social revolution stands the figure of a man so "controversial" thirty years after his death that within his own country his name is expunged from the record of the revolution he led, while except for a small idolatrous segment, the revolutionary movement generally has not begun to assimilate his contribution to revolutionary theory, nor come to terms with his revolutionary role. The progenitor of virtually all revolutionary Marxist critiques of Communist revolutions and revolutionary states, vilified by Stalin as a renegade, counterrevolutionary wrecker, and Fascist agent, and eventually murdered by his henchmen, Leon Trotsky was in reality one of the most extraordinary revolutionary figures of all time.

In order to lend persuasiveness to the comments that follow, it should be noted that the present writer in no way regards himself as a "Trotskyist." Further, he considers the sterility of organized Trotskyism to be an integral part of the tragedy of international Marxism in the epoch of the Russian Revolution and its aftermath. In its long, intimate polarization with Stalinism, for example, the main Trotskyist movement in the United States (YSA-SWP) has come to practice a politics which bears uncanny resemblance to the politics of the Communist Party, U.S.A., in the heyday of its anti-Trotsky fervor. Most ironic of all is the YSA-SWP's enthronement of the principle of "ideological homogeneity" as a doctrine of party orthodoxy, since this was the essence of Stalinism's original triumph over Trotskyism: to render all organized dissent within the Communist movement *heresy,* and by so doing establish that monolithic frame which became its hallmark, and which destroyed the ability of the international revolutionary movement to think and theorize, and ultimately to develop its praxis as a revolutionary vanguard.

The only significant actor in the Russian October of 1917 to play a major role in the revolution of 1905, Leon Trotsky personally contributed more to the Bolshevik conquest of power than any other Bolshevik leader with the exception of Lenin. So, far from being an alien in the ranks, as Stalinist historians have portrayed him, Trotsky was a man whose extraordinary talents and genius were matched by such utter integrity of purpose and dedication to the revolution that, in the midst of the civil war, Lenin authorized him, as organizer and head of the Red Army, to issue without prior consultation or approval any order that he deemed necessary to defend the Bolshevik regime.

It was Trotsky who, as a brilliant orator and the president of the key Petrograd Soviet (a post to which he was elected both in 1905 and 1917), mobilized the mass support for the Bolshevik Party. Trotsky's part in these historic days has been summarized by Sukhanov, a non-Bolshevik eyewitness of the events: "Tearing himself from the work in revolutionary headquarters he would fly from the Obukhovsky factory to the Trubocheny, from the Putilov to the Baltic shipyard, from the Riding Academy to the barracks, and seemed to be speaking simultaneously in all places. Every Petrograd worker and soldier knew him and heard him personally. His influence—both in the masses and in headquarters—was overwhelming. He was the central figure of those days, and the chief hero of this remarkable page of history."

If his public activity were the sum of Trotsky's role in the October Revolution, it alone would have ranked him as one of its most important figures. But it was, in a sense, only the beginning of his contribution. It is one thing to be a popular leader, a *vox populi* giving expression to the pent-up sufferings and rage of previously silent masses, inspiring this new social force to seize the historical hour and redress epochal grievances and injustice. It is quite another, however, to be the leader of a vanguard party.

Behind the scenes, in the highest councils of the Bolshevik Party, while Lenin was in hiding, it was Trotsky who carried the fight to endorse Lenin's summons to insurrection. The opposition to the proposed seizure of power was formidable, and at first included not only Zinoviev and Kamenev, but the bulk of the party leadership. Furthermore, when the struggle was won, it was Trotsky who emerged as the master tactician of the actual insurrection. For Trotsky was president of the Petrograd Soviet, the very center of the popular revolutionary power, and as head of the Military Revolutionary Committee of the Bolshevik Party, it was he who chose the timing and determined the tactics of the insurrection, planned its strategy, and carried it to its successful conclusion.

To seize power was an extraordinary accomplishment, but to hold power was even more difficult. The fledgling regime was internationally isolated by the failures of the European revolutions, and domestically weakened by four years of world war. Now it was faced not only by the revolt of the disinherited classes of the old order, but by the military intervention of the dominant capitalist world powers as well. In this new struggle, which was to last three interminable and extremely bloody years, Trotsky's role was again unparalleled. For it was he who created and organized the Red Army, and, as its commander, led it to victory.

With victory, and the consolidation of Bolshevik power, the second phase of Trotsky's career began. It was this phase that produced the epochal controversy over "Trotskyism," which persists to this day. From 1923 to 1929 Trotsky was the principal leader of the Bolshevik internal oppositions, which developed in the face of policies undertaken by the regime that seemed to depart from the traditions of Marxism and Bolshevism, and the revolutionary program of October, 1917. These oppositions eventually came to include most of the figures of the "Old Guard" of Lenin's party, including Zinoviev and Kamenev, who had at first sided with Stalin against Trotsky.

After 1929, the year of his exile and the consolidation of Stalin's absolute dominance of the party, Trotsky became the sole voice opposing Stalin's policies among the original revolutionary leadership. "Throughout these twelve years, from 1929–1940," writes Trotsky's biographer Isaac Deutscher, "no voice could be raised against Stalin in the USSR; and not even an echo could be heard of the earlier intense struggles, except in the grovelling confessions of guilt to which so many of Stalin's adversaries had been reduced. Consequently, Trotsky appeared to stand quite alone against Stalin's autocracy. It was as if a huge historic conflict had become compressed into a controversy and feud between two men."

To what extent the policies of Stalin were "betrayals" of the revolutionary ideals, and to what extent they were necessary accommodations to the social situation in which the revolution found itself, constitute the essence of the controversy over Trotskyism. The issues span the entire range of modern revolutionary problems, including the relation between national struggles and the international revolution, between revolutionary administrations and the laboring classes, between revolutionary democracy and revolutionary stability, between the efforts to promote the growth of the forces of material production and the need to develop revolutionary consciousness in the new order. Every significant Marxist (and even non-Marxist) critique of Communist practice in these areas, from that of Mao Tse-tung to Fidel Castro and Che Guevara, owes a debt to Trotsky's analysis in his polemic against Stalin. His was not only the first major attempt to come to grips with these questions, but in many ways is still the most penetrating and profound.

On the other hand, his mistakes, both theoretical and practical, were serious and must not be overlooked. Among the most important was the too simple analogy he drew between the bankruptcy of the Second International and that of the Third, and his parallel reduction of the crisis of the revolutionary movement in the Stalin period to that of a crisis of revolutionary leadership. This he felt could be cured by the creation of a new international, guided by the classical principles of Bolshevism under Lenin. Within this framework of analysis, however, there is no way to explain adequately the triumph of the Yugoslav, Chinese, and Vietnamese revolutions, which followed World War II, under Stalinist auspices. The fact that they were led by maverick Stalinists (and opposed by Stalin) does not resolve the dilemma; if

Stalinism could produce mavericks like Mao, Ho, and Tito—who were all in turn opposed by *their* domestic Trotskyists—then wherein lay the necessity of a Fourth International? At the very least, it is impossible to sustain the political parallel between the Communist International and the International Social Democracy that is so central to Trotskyism.

All this is not to say that the heart of Trotsky's criticisms of the policies of the Comintern—in Spain, in Germany, in China—were not correct: by and large they were. It is only to underscore the importance of viewing Trotsky's critique as a necessary point of departure for analysis, and not an adequate theory and program in itself. One should avoid the temptation, in short, to accept and defend the entire viewpoint of a man who is admittedly one of the most brilliant and most appealing revolutionary figures of modern times.

Fortunately, there exist two treatments of the Stalin-Trotsky controversy in its historical context which are free from polemical distortion and idolatry, while at the same time presenting different perspectives on the main dialectical drama. These are E. H. Carr's *History of Soviet Russia* (10 volumes) and Isaac Deutscher's monumental trilogy, *The Prophet Armed, The Prophet Unarmed,* and *The Prophet Outcast.* These volumes provide ample background to the interested student of these issues, and to the renewal of the debate which appears in the present text.

Trotsky: The Great Debate Renewed, which consists of a series of essays originally appearing in the pages of *New Left Review,* is in more than one respect itself a significant event in this history. It represents the first time in the English-speaking world (and perhaps anywhere) that a Marxist, but non-Trotskyist, journal opened its pages to a serious consideration of Trotsky's ideas. It remains to this day, moreover, the only extended polemic on these questions. Happily, moreover, as a polemic it is carried out on a very high level. Nicolas Krassó, a former student of Georg Lukács, was a participant in the Hungarian Revolution of 1956, and is an editor of *New Left Review.* Ernest Mandel, a leading Trotskyist and internationally renowned Marxist theoretician in his own right, is the author of *Marxist Economic Theory* (2 vols.), *Europe vs. America,* and *The Formation of the Economic Thought of Karl Marx.* Their debate encompasses the role of the revolutionary party, the relation of national to international revolution, and the principal problems of the postrevolutionary social order: in short, both the main themes of the original controversy and the main questions that face the revolution today. Revolutionaries ready to take seriously the task of reevaluating the past in order to create solid foundations for a revolutionary theory of the present would do well to begin their effort with this volume.

David Horowitz
Editor, *Ramparts* Magazine

Preface

Four years have now passed since I wrote "Trotsky's Marxism" but nothing that has happened in this period has altered my conviction that an assessment of Trotsky's contribution to Marxism remains a vital task for the revolutionary movement. Whether his theses were correct or incorrect, he was one of the few major Marxist thinkers who attempted a scientific evaluation of the political issues raised by the ascendancy of Stalin in the international Communist movement. His ideas on a whole range of issues, from the dual nature of the Soviet state to the class dynamics of the anti-imperialist struggle, from the nature of socialist democracy to the forms of the revolution in the imperialist countries themselves, remain crucial poles of reference in debates between revolutionaries. The original publication by *New Left Review* of "Trotsky's Marxism" and of the exchanges that it provoked was an acknowledgment that the new wave of revolutionaries in the West needed to take up again the debates on these questions that Stalin had terminated so brutally. The polemic is published here in its original form without other than minor stylistic changes. I have also included Chris Arthur's discussion of the nature of the Soviet Union, since it arose indirectly out of the exchange between Ernest Mandel and myself, concentrating on an aspect of the discussion that had been relatively neglected by us. I hope that the reader will find that publication in this form affords an insight into the developing views of the participants and more than compensates for the lack of formal tidiness and completeness.

N. K.

London, November, 1970

Contents

TROTSKY
The Great Debate Renewed

NICOLAS KRASSÓ

Trotsky's Marxism

For many years, Trotsky was an impossible subject for a Marxist. The struggle in the Bolshevik party in the twenties produced such a violent polarization of his image within the international working-class movement that all rational discussion of his person and works ceased. The anathema pronounced by Stalin made his name synonymous with treason for millions of militants all over the world. On the other side of the divide, a dedicated and segregated minority sanctified his memory, and believed his thought to be the "Leninism of our time." Even today, thirty years after his death and a decade after the death of Stalin, there is still a taboo on normal discussion of Trotsky within the Communist movement. Magical attitudes toward his figure continue—a striking anachronism in the world of today. The one exception to this rule is, of course, Isaac Deutscher's three-volume biography—itself only a part of a larger *oeuvre*. But here, paradoxically, the greatness of Deutscher's achievement has seemingly overpowered any other potential contributors to a debate, within Marxism, on Trotsky's true historical role. It is surely significant that there has never been any Marxist appraisal of Deutscher's work of a quality that matched its stature. It has been so much in advance of contemporary attitudes that it has not yet been properly assimilated, and hence has never been contested. Its implications, however, will only be assimilated by a continuous discussion of different areas within Soviet history—even where divergent views are developed. It would be an error not to broach specific problems for fear of failing to come to grips with the whole revolutionary epic or with its historian.

The aim of this essay is to approach such a problem: how should we judge Trotsky as a Marxist? This means comparing him with Lenin (rather than with Stalin) and trying to see what is the specific unity of his theoretical writings and his practice as a politician. For this purpose, Trotsky's life falls into four distinct phases: 1879–1917, 1917–21, 1921–29, and 1929–40. It will be the thesis of this essay that all four periods are best understood in the framework of a single problem: Trotsky's relation to the party as the revolutionary organization of the proletariat, and its latent theoretical foundations. This focus, it will be argued, illuminates all the basic characteristics (vices and virtues) of Trotsky's thought as a Marxist, and explains the vicissitudes of his political career.

1879–1917

"Lenin's Cudgel" to Founder-Member Menshevik

Before the October Revolution, Trotsky was never a disciplined member of any faction of the Russian Social Democratic Party, Bolshevik or Menshevik. This record may be explained partly by political disagreements at different conjunctures with the Bolsheviks and the Mensheviks. But it also undoubtedly reflected a deeper theoretical option, which governed his actions in this period. One of his first recorded writings, Deutscher tells us, was an essay on party organization produced in Siberia. In this, Trotsky argued for a ruthless disciplinary control over the revolutionary movement by a strong Central Committee. "The Central Committee will cut off its relations with (any undisciplined organization) and it will thereby cut off that organization from the entire world revolution," he wrote.[1] It was consistent with this

[1] Isaac Deutscher, *The Prophet Armed: Trotsky 1879–1921* (Oxford University Press, 1954), p. 45.

view that Trotsky, when he left Russia in 1902, should have initially advocated an iron disciplinary system in the dispute between Iskra and the Economists at the Third Congress of the RSDP in Brussels in July, 1903. The party's statutes, he argued, should express "the leadership's organized distrust" of the members, a distrust exercised by vigilant, vertical control over the party.

This formulation is visibly different in spirit from anything that is to be found in *What Is to Be Done?* (New York: International Publishers, 1943). Trotsky in this phase, just emerged from exile and new to the national revolutionary movement, was known as "Lenin's cudgel," but if we compare the writings of the two at this period, it is clear, as we shall see, that Trotsky's "proto-Bolshevik" phase merely reproduced the external and formal aspects of Lenin's theory of party organization—without its sociological content—and thus necessarily caricatured it as a militarized hierarchy of command, a conception completely foreign to Lenin. Since it was not founded on any organic theory of the revolutionary party, there is nothing surprising about the fact that Trotsky suddenly switched to the opposite extreme at the same Congress, eventually denouncing Lenin as the "party's disorganizer" and the architect of a plan to turn the RSDP into a band of conspirators rather than of the Russian working class. "Lenin's cudgel" thus became a founder-member of the Mensheviks in late 1903. In April, 1904, Trotsky published in Geneva "Our Political Tasks," an essay dedicated to the Menshevik Axelrod. In this, he frontally rejected Lenin's whole theory of the revolutionary party, explicitly denying Lenin's fundamental thesis that socialism as a theory had to be brought to the working class from the outside, through a party that included the revolutionary intelligentsia. Trotsky attacked this theory as "substitutionism" and he denounced it in lurid fashion: "Lenin's methods lead to this: the party organization at first substitutes itself for the party as a whole; then the Central Committee substitutes itself for the organization; and finally a single 'dictator' substitutes himself for the Central Committee." He went on to denounce Lenin for "malicious and morally repulsive suspiciousness." [2]

---

[2] Isaac Deutscher, *The Prophet Armed*, pp. 90, 92.

Party and Class

His own model of the social democratic party was borrowed from the German party and implied a party coextensive with the working class. The obvious criticism of such a formulation, in a Marxist perspective, is that the true problems of revolutionary theory, and the relations between party and class, cannot be approached scientifically with the concept of "substitution" and its implied opposite "identity." Party and class pertain to different levels of the social structure, and the relationship between them is always one of articulation. No exchange ("substitution") is possible between them, just as no identity between them is possible; for they are necessarily different instances of a stratified social ensemble, not comparable or equivalent expressions of a given level of it. The speculative concepts of "substitution" or "identity" *ab initio* preclude any accurate understanding of the specific nature of the practice of the revolutionary party on (and in) the working class, as Lenin theorized it. They amount to a radical failure to see the inevitably autonomous role of political institutions in general, and the revolutionary party in particular—autonomous in relation to mass forces within a social formation determined in the last instance, of course, by the economy.

The failure to grasp the specificity of political organizations and the role of the revolutionary party—in other words, the lack of a theory of the party—explains the sudden and arbitrary changes in Trotsky's attitudes toward party organization in these years. They merely had a psychological meaning—expressions of an ambivalence between "authoritarian" and "libertarian" attitudes (later reproduced in the sudden changes from his attitudes to War Communism to his role in combating "bureaucracy") whose abstract opposition itself indicated a pre-Marxist problem. They had no theoretical status proper—beyond this indication of an absence, a blank zone, in Trotsky's thought.

This absence, however, was linked to a peculiarly intense intuition of mass social forces as such. In late 1904, Trotsky seceded from the Menshevik faction and went into intellectual partnership with Parvus, a Russian émigré in the German SDP. The extreme instability of his links to any organizational grouping was thus rapidly confirmed. It was this unanchored position, however, which paradoxically made possible his meteoric ascent in the 1905 Revolution—a spontaneous eruption over which no revolutionary organization had time to gain effective control, before it dissipated its momentum and was defeated. Both Bolsheviks and Mensheviks were taken by surprise by the revolution, and their leaders arrived in Russia only with some delay. Trotsky, who was in St. Petersburg from the beginning, adapted much more quickly to the mass upsurge of October, unstructured as it was by any guiding political party. He soon won leadership of the St. Petersburg Soviet. Deutscher correctly observes that precisely in this success, "he embodied the immaturity of the movement." This immaturity, of course, produced the rapid and decisive defeat of the revolution five months later—the funeral of spontaneity in the history of the Russian working-class movement.

"Results and Prospects"

However, it was this experience that crystallized the first and most important of all Trotsky's writings, *Results and Prospects,* written in jail in 1906. This work contains all the elements of the later views set forth in a polemical pamphlet of 1928, *Permanent Revolution,* but it is much more than this. It is unquestionably a brilliant prefiguration of the main class characteristics of the October Revolution of 1917.

> In a country economically backward, the proletariat can take power earlier than in countries where capitalism is advanced. . . . The Russian revolution produces conditions, in which power may . . . pass to the proletariat before the politicians of bourgeois liberalism have had a chance to show their statesman-like genius properly. . . . The proletariat in power will appear before the peasantry as its liberator.[3]

"Permanent Revolution"

Trotsky correctly predicted that the atomization of the peasantry and the weakness of the bourgeoisie in Russia would make possible the seizure of power by the working class while it was still a minority of the nation. Once in power, it would have to win

---

[3] Leon Trotsky, *Results and Prospects,* p. 195.

the support of the peasantry at all costs, and would be obliged to move from "democratic" to "socialist" measures without any hiatus between the two. He called this process "permanent revolution"—an inept designation that indicated the lack of scientific precision even in his profoundest insights. By evoking the idea of a continuous conflagration at all times and all places—a metaphysical carnival of insurrection—it lent itself to distortion in the polemic of both Trotsky's opponents and his followers. The romantic-idealist character of the formula inevitably generated critical errors in Trotsky's own thoughts, even at this date. Above all, this formula conflated the two quite distinct problems of the class character of the coming revolution in Russia (uninterrupted progression from democratic to socialist demands) and the ability of the Russian revolution to maintain itself internationally. For in this essay Trotsky repeatedly proclaimed the impossibility of the revolution in Russia resisting counterrevolutionary assault without the assistance of simultaneous revolutions in Western Europe. The "logic" of this assumption derived from the confused verbalism of "permanent revolution"—a formula that allowed Trotsky to move from the national character of the revolution in Russia to the international conditions of its survival as if they were so many steps on a single escalator, "permanently" moving upward. The illegitimate nature of this procedure is all too obvious, and vitiated Trotsky's theses fundamentally. This does not detract from the magnitude of his achievements in correctly forecasting the basic nature of the October Revolution eleven years before it occurred, at a time when no other Russian leader had rejected the classic predictions of Georgy Plekhanov. It merely situates this achievement within the specific coordinates of Trotsky's Marxism.

The Absence of the Party

Results and Prospects is an extraordinary essay in class analysis. It is no less extraordinary in its lack of any analysis of the role of political organization in the socialist struggle. The party, once again, is quite absent from Trotsky's scenario of the future revolution. When he discusses the prerequisites of socialism (planned production, dominance of large-scale factories, and dictatorship of the proletariat), he nowhere mentions the party or its role. He attacks Blanquists and anarchists, but then merely says: "Social Democrats speak of the conquest of power as the conscious action of the revolutionary class." [4] Its vanguard has been forgotten.

The only discussion of parties in the whole one-hundred-page essay is a single, perceptive criticism of the social democratic parties of the West, which was an accurate comment on these organizations, but whose general application implied a complete hostility to the very existence of a revolutionary party.[5] Indeed, when Trotsky writes of the political struggle in Russia, he never simply refers to the role of revolutionary organizations—he only speaks of social forces.

One other comment on this premonitory work should be made. There is patent unawareness of the problems of the party in it. By contrast, Trotsky shows a great awareness of the *state* as a bureaucratic and military apparatus. There is a long and graphic account of the historical role of the Russian state in the formation of modern Russian society. Trotsky borrowed much of this analysis from the liberal historian Paul Miliukov, and from his partner Parvus. But the eloquence of this excursus throws into sharp relief his parallel silence on the party. This polarity was not accidental, and it reemerged in a crucial practical context in a later phase.

The immediate consequences of this critical absence in Trotsky's thought, however, became concretely evident after his release from jail. From 1907 to 1914, Trotsky's political record was one of intermittent and unavailing efforts to bring the opposed social democratic factions together, for which purpose he eventually formed the unprincipled and short-lived August Bloc. He played no part whatever in the decisive work of building the Bolshevik party, undertaken by Lenin in these years. He thus never gained the experience of party life, which his contemporaries Joseph Stalin, Grigory Zinoviev, and Nikolai Bukharin

[4] *Ibid.,* p. 229.
[5] *Ibid.,* p. 246.

accumulated in this formative period. Deutscher comments accurately:

> The years between 1907 and 1914 form in his life a chapter
> singularly devoid of political achievement. . . . His writings . . .
> consisted of brilliant journalism and literary criticism, but did
> not include a single significant work on political theory. . . . In
> these years, however, Lenin, assisted by his followers, was forg-
> ing his party, and men like Zinoviev, Kamenev, Bukharin and,
> later, Stalin were growing to a stature which enabled them to
> play leading parts within the party in 1917. To the stature which
> Trotsky had attained in 1904–1906 the present period added
> little or nothing.[6]

"The Intelligentsia and Socialism"

It would be a mistake, however, to think that Trotsky produced no important writings in this long interlude. He wrote one
crucial essay that illuminates the latent axes of his political thought
with particular clarity. This was "The Intelligentsia and Socialism,"
written in 1910. In it, Trotsky shows a bitter hostility toward
intellectuals, inside and outside the socialist movement. This hostility was a reflection of his notion of the intelligentsia. It is evident, from his writings, that Trotsky saw intellectuals in a wholly
pre-Leninist manner, as individuals of bourgeois origin concerned
with "ideas" or "literature," and essentially divorced from the
proletariat and political struggle. The basic image of the intellectual in his work is always that of the salon *littérateur*. Now
this image is precisely that cultivated by the bourgeoisie itself—
which has segregated "art" and "thought" from "mundane" activities (such as economics and politics), diffused the ideal of the
intellectual as one devoted to the remote, esoteric pursuit of
these. Moreover, the vulgar anti-intellectualism of an *ouvrierist* or
Laborist working class is the mirror image of this bourgeois conception: the "intellectual" becomes a pejorative category indicating a dilettante, parasite, or renegade. This nexus of conceptions, of course, has nothing whatever to do with Marxism. But it
explains why Trotsky's apparent approximation to Lenin's position on party organization in 1903 was so formal and external. For

---

[6] Isaac Deutscher, *The Prophet Armed*, p. 176.

Lenin's theory of party organization—in *What Is to Be Done?*
—was inseparable from his theory of the role and nature of
intellectuals in a revolutionary party. The essence of this was
that: (1) intellectuals of bourgeois origin are indispensable to the
constitution of a revolutionary party—they alone enable the working class to master scientific socialism; (2) the work of the revolutionary party abolishes the distinction between "intellectuals"
and "workers" within its ranks. Antonio Gramsci, of course, developed Lenin's theory in his famous analysis of the revolutionary
party as the "Modern Prince," all of whose members become
intellectuals of a new type.

This complex conception contrasts with Trotsky's acceptance
of traditional categories and the prejudices that went with them.
When writing of intellectuals, he was thinking of the esoteric
literary circles in Moscow whom he was later to attack in *Literature and Revolution* (University of Michigan Press, 1960)—
never of the new intellectuals forged in and through the Bolshevik
party, as its members. In a word, he lacked any Marxist theory of
intellectuals and their relation to the revolutionary movement, and
so was left with mere attitudes. In his essay of 1910, he states
flatly that as the socialist movement in Europe grows, fewer
and fewer intellectuals join it. This law is true of students as well:
"Throughout their entire history . . . the students of Europe have
been merely the sensitive barometer of the bourgeois classes." [7]
The nub of his analysis of the relationship between intellectuals
and the working class is a sweeping dismissal of the former, which
showed the extent of his failure to assimilate *What Is to Be
Done?* [8] He writes: "If the actual conquest of the apparatus of
society depended on the previous coming over of the intelligentsia
to the party of the European proletariat, then the prospects of
collectivism would be wretched indeed." Given this general
standpoint, it is clear why his brief "centralism" of 1903 was
mechanical and brittle. It was a parody of Leninism—a militarized mimicry of its discipline, without its internal meaning—
the transformation of "workers" and "intellectuals" into *revolu-*

---

[7] "The Intelligentsia and Socialism."

[8] Lenin's theory of the revolutionary party was not, of course, completely developed in *What Is to Be Done?* His mature theory only crystallized after the 1905 Revolution, in the practice of party construction.

tionaries by a unified political practice. The only political role
Trotsky ever accorded to intellectuals was that of "substitutionism," in an essay specifically on the Russian intelligentsia.[9]
Decembrists, Narodniks, and Marxists were indifferently condemned as groups substituting themselves for the social classes
they claimed to represent, in what Deutscher calls a "gloomy
survey" of Russian history. Once again, the lack of any theory of
differentiated levels or instances of the social structure leads to
the notion of a horizontal exchange between "intellectuals" and
"classes" in which a substitution of one by the other is possible.
Thus the only entry of the intellectuals into politics is necessarily
a usurpation: it can only be at the expense of the proletariat.
What is missing, once again, is the idea of the party as an autonomous structure that recombines and transforms two differential
phenomena—the intelligentsia and the working class. Within this
conception, it makes no sense to talk of "substituting" one
element for another, since they are not commensurable to be interchangeable. They are *modifiable*—in a new political practice,
which is a revolutionary party.

Trotsky's history before 1917 may thus be summed up as
follows. He was always a *franc-tireur* outside the organized ranks
of the working-class movement. He showed a unique intuitive insight into the class character of the forces that were gathering for
the Russian revolution. But this was coupled with a profound and
consistent failure to understand the nature and role of a revolutionary party—a failure linked to his pre-Marxist conception of
theory and organizations. As late as 1915, the belief that the party
was an arbitrary epiphenomenon in the class struggle is patent in
his writing:

> Between the position of a party and the interests of the social
> stratum on which it rests, there may be a certain lack of harmony
> that may later become converted into a profound contradiction.
> The conduct of a party may change under the influence of the
> temper of the masses. This is indisputable. All the more reason
> therefore for us, in our calculations, *to cease relying on less
> stable and less trustworthy elements such as the slogans and the
> tactics of a party,* and to refer to more stable historical factors:

---

[9] *The Prophet Armed,* pp. 187 ff.

to the social structure of the nation, to the relation of class forces and the tendencies of development.[10]

This incomprehension of the role of the Leninist party explains his abstention from any participation in the crucial formation of the Bolshevik party from 1907 on. He himself later characterized his attitude in this phase with great honesty and accuracy:

> I never endeavored to create a grouping on the basis of the ideas of permanent revolution. My inner-party stand was a conciliationist one, and when at certain moments I strove for the formation of groupings, then it was precisely on this basis. *My conciliationism flowed from a sort of social-revolutionary fatalism.* I believed that the logic of the class struggle would compel both factions to pursue the same revolutionary line. The great historical significance of Lenin's policy was still unclear to me at that time, his policy of irreconcilable ideological demarcation and, when necessary, split, for the purpose of welding and tempering the core of the truly revolutionary revolutionary party. . . . In all the most important cases, where I placed myself in contradiction to Lenin tactically and organizationally, right was on his side.[11]

It is now possible to locate the specific theoretical deviation latent in Trotsky's thought. Traditionally, Marxism has been constantly subject to the deformation called "economism." This is the reduction of all other levels of a social formation to the movement of the economy, which becomes an idealist "essence," of which social groups, political institutions, and cultural products are merely "manifestations." This deviation, with all its practical political consequences, was widespread in the Second International. It was characteristic of the Right, which dominated the International. What has been less noticed is that the Left of the

---

[10] *The Struggle for Power* (my italics). Trotsky's attitude to the party in these years may be compared with Rosa Luxemburg's. Luxemburg was aware of the revisionism of the German party well before Lenin, but failed to split the SPD and thus delayed the work of constructing a revolutionary party. The consequences were fatal—the defeat of the Spartakist insurrection of 1918. Both Trotsky and Luxemburg relied on the revolutionary élan of the masses at the expense of consideration of the problem of its mobilization in a revolutionary organization.

[11] *Permanent Revolution*, p. 49.

International often exhibited an analogous deviation. We may call this, for the sake of convenience, "sociologism." Here it is not the economy, but *social classes,* which are extracted from the complex historical totality and hypostasized in an idealist fashion as the demiurges of any given political situation. Class struggle becomes the immediate, internal "truth" of any political event, and mass forces become the exclusive historical agents. Economism naturally leads to passivity and tailism; sociologism, on the contrary, tends to lead to voluntarism. Luxemburg represents the extreme logic of this tendency within the Second International, where it takes the form of an explicit exaltation of spontaneity. Trotsky represents a different variant of this current, but the fundamental tenet is parallel. In his writings, mass forces are presented as constantly dominant in society, without any political organizations or institutions intervening as necessary and permanent levels of the social formation. Lenin's Marxism, by contrast, is defined by the notion of a complex totality, in which all the levels—economic, social, political, and ideological—are always operational, and there is a permutation of the main locus of contradictions between them. Trotsky's extrapolation of mass forces from this complex tier of levels was the ultimate source of his theoretical mistakes, both before and after the revolution.

1917–21

Statesman

The eruption of the February Revolution transformed the political relationships within the Russian social democratic movement. The new situation suddenly freed Trotsky from his past. Within a few months, he had abandoned his Menshevik associates and aligned himself with Bolshevik positions. He now emerged as a great revolutionary. This was the heroic phase of his life, when he captured the imagination of the world as the architect of the October insurrection and the military commander of the Civil War. Not only this: he was the supreme orator of the revolution. In his person, he was both Danton and Carnot—the great people's tribune and the great military leader of the Russian revolution. As such, Trotsky was exactly the kind of man most observers abroad, whether sympathetic or hostile, imagined a revolutionary to be. He seemed the incarnation of continuity between the French and Russian revolutions. Lenin, by contrast, was an apparently prosaic man—altogether different from the declamatory heroes of 1789. He represented a new type of revolutionary. The difference between the two men was fundamental, and is visible throughout the period when they worked so closely together. Trotsky never wholly acclimatized himself within the Bolshevik party. In July, 1917, he was parachuted onto the summit of the Bolshevik organization, its Central Committee, without any experience in party life or party practice. He was thus always perceived very differently within its ranks, from without. His international image never coincided with his internal party image; he was always to some extent suspected as a latecomer and intruder. It is significant that as late as 1928, in the midst of the inner-party struggle, his colleague and ally Evgeny Preobrazhensky could speak of "We Old Bolsheviks" to distinguish his position from those of Trotsky. He was certainly never quite accepted by the Old Bolsheviks as one of them. This separate role is evident in the revolution and Civil War itself. Trotsky was the dynamo of the militarized Bolshevik state, when it was on a war footing. He was not a party man with any responsibility for the maintenance and mobilization of party organization in these years. Indeed, he was criticized by many Bolsheviks for policies within the army that were actually hostile to the party as such. Thus Trotsky was determined to strengthen the power of professional military officers with a czarist past in the Red Army, and he fought the imposition of control over them by political commissars appointed by the party. The dispute over this issue—in which Trotsky already clashed with Joseph Stalin and Kliment Voroshilov—was a major controversy at the Eighth Party Congress in 1919. Lenin supported Trotsky, but resentment in the party against him was evident in the secret instructions passed at the Congress. Anastas Mikoyan's cry at the Twelfth Congress was thus an accurate reflection of how he was perceived by the permanent staff of the party; "Trotsky is a man of state, not of the party!" [12]

The nature of Trotsky's talent as an orator was complementary to his talent as a military commander. Both were exclusive of a specifically party practice. An organizer of a political party has to persuade individuals or groups to accept the policies he advocates and his authority to implement them. This requires great patience and the ability to maneuver intelligently within a complex political struggle, in which the actors are equally equipped for discussion and decision. This ability is quite different from that of the mass orator. Trotsky had an extraordinary gift for communication with crowds. But the nature of his appeal to them was necessarily emotional—a great transmission of urgency and militancy. As a public speaker, however, he enjoyed a quite unilateral relationship with these crowds—he harangued them for determinate ends, to mobilize them in the struggle against counterrevolution. His military gift was parallel in character. He was not an organizer of the party—he had no experience of how a party actually worked, and he did not seem to be particularly interested in such questions. He did, however, achieve the feat of creating a Red Army of five million men in two years, from virtually nothing, and leading it to victory against the White Armies and their foreign allies. His organizational ability was thus essentially voluntarist in character. He had authority *ab initio* to organize the Army; as People's Commissar for War he had all the prestige of Lenin and the Soviet state behind him. He did not have to *win* this authority in a political arena by persuading his peers to accept him. It was the authority of military command and its power to enforce strict obedience. The affinity between the war commander and the popular tribune is thus quite explicable. In both cases, Trotsky's role was implicitly voluntarist. As a public speaker he had to make an emotional appeal to mobilize the masses for precise purposes; as a pillar of the Soviet state he had to give orders to his subordinates for precise purposes. His task in either role was to ensure the means to a previously determined end. This is a different task from that of ensuring that

---

[12] Isaac Deutscher, *The Prophet Unarmed: Trotsky 1921–1929* (Oxford University Press, 1959), p. 32.

a novel end prevails among various competing opinions in a political organization. The voluntarist is in his element haranguing crowds or dispatching troops, but these roles should not be confused with the ability to lead a revolutionary party.

From Military to Economic Problems

By 1921, the Civil War was won. With victory, the Bolshevik party had to switch its whole orientation from military to economic problems. Reconstruction and reorganization of the Soviet economy were now its main strategic objectives. Trotsky's adaptation to the new situation revealed how consistent his whole political practice was in this phase. He simply proposed the imposition of military solutions on economic problems—calling for an intensified War Communism and the introduction of forced labor. This extraordinary episode was not just a parenthesis or aberration in his career. It had profound theoretical and practical sources in his past. His role as People's Commissar for War predisposed him to an economic policy that was conceived as a straightforward military mobilization: he was merely extending his previous practice in advocating it. At the same time his propensity for a "command" solution undoubtedly reflected his incomprehension of the specific role of the party and his consequent tendency to seek political solutions at the level of the *state*. Indeed, his slogan in the trade union debate of 1921 was explicitly "statification" of the trade unions. Trotsky also argued for a competent, permanent bureaucracy with some material privileges; for this Stalin was later to call him the "coryphée of the bureaucrats."

Moreover, Trotsky did not justify forced labor as a regrettable necessity imposed by the political conjuncture, the temporary product of an emergency. He tried to legitimate it *sub specie aeternitatis,* explaining that in all societies labor was compulsory —only the forms of compulsion varied. He combined this flat advocacy of coercion with an exalted mystique of social dedication, urging work brigades to sing socialist hymns as they toiled.

> Display untiring energy in your work, as if you were on the march or in battle. A deserter from labor is as contemptible and despicable as a deserter from the battlefield. Severe punishment

to both! . . . Begin and complete your work, wherever possible, to the sound of socialist hymns and songs. Your work is not slave labor but high service to the socialist fatherland.[13]

This contradictory amalgam was united, of course, by the equal voluntarism of both notions: the economy as a coercive command or as a mystical service.

Trotsky was initially able to win Lenin's support for his plans for the militarization of labor. But after the great debate on the trade unions in 1921 and the termination of the Polish War, his bid for a wide-scale purge of the trade unions' elected representatives was sharply repudiated by Lenin. The Central Committee of the party publicly denounced "militarized and bureaucratic" forms of work. Trotsky's policies were thus rejected by the Bolsheviks, amidst a general revulsion against him as the ideologue of War Communism. The outcome of the economic debate marked the distance between Lenin's idea of a highly disciplined party and Trotsky's advocacy of a militarily organized state.

1921–29

Oppositionist

The inner-party struggle of the twenties was obviously the central phase of Trotsky's life. The events of a few years were decisive for world history for decades to come. These decisions were taken by very few people. It is not often that such decisions gain universal significance. What was Trotsky's role in the fateful drama of the twenties?

The struggle for dominance of the Bolshevik party must to some extent be separated from the political issues that provoked

---

[13] *The Prophet Armed,* p. 495. This image recalls the Jesuit of Paraguay. Trotsky was later to write that the reason that bourgeois philistines detested Jesuits so much was that they were the soldiers of the Church, whereas most priests were merely its shopkeepers. It is, of course, true that there is no reason to make any discrimination between the two. Trotsky, however, seems to have preferred Jesuits to other priests. It is clear that in a revolutionary period, a socialist militant will be nearer a soldier than a shopkeeper in outlook; but should this temporary state of affairs lead any socialist to forget that the military outlook is no less a product of class society than a mercantile outlook?

it. For much of the time the conflict in the party focused on the exercise of power as such—within the context, of course, of the ideological disputes of the contending groups. It will be seen, in fact, that an overideological reading of the inner-party situation was one of Trotsky's most serious theoretical and political mistakes. It will thus be convenient to divide consideration of the twenties into two levels: that of the political-tactical struggle itself, and that of the ideological and strategic debate over the destiny of the revolution.

The Political-Tactical Struggle

From 1921 on, Trotsky was isolated at the summit of the Bolshevik party. It is important to emphasize that the struggle against Trotsky was initially a resistance by virtually the whole Old Guard of the Bolsheviks against the possibility of Trotsky succeeding Lenin. This is what explains the unanimity with which all the other leaders in the Politburo—Grigory Zinoviev, Leo Kamenev, Joseph Stalin, Mikhail Kalinin, and Mikhail Tomsky —opposed him in Lenin's own lifetime. Trotsky seemed to be the outstanding revolutionary leader after Lenin. Yet he was not a historic member of the party, and he was widely distrusted within it. His military prominence and his role in the trade union debates seemed to throw a shadow of potential Bonapartism across the political landscape. Lenin himself evinced no special confidence in him. This was the situation that allowed Stalin in 1923, the last year of Lenin's life, to win control of the party machine and, with it, of general political power in the U.S.S.R.

It is evident that Trotsky did not see what was happening in these years. He thought Zinoviev and Kamenev were more important than Stalin, and failed to understand the significance of the new role of the General Secretary. This extraordinary lack of lucidity may be contrasted with Lenin's acute awareness, even in his illness, of the drift of events. In December, 1922, he drafted his notes on nationalities, denouncing Stalin and Feliks Dzerzhinsky with unprecedented violence for their repression in Georgia. Lenin forwarded these notes to Trotsky with a specific instruction to force the issue to a decisive resolution at the Central Committee. Trotsky ignored his request; he believed that Lenin had exaggerated the matter greatly. A month later, Lenin wrote his famous "will," in which it is quite clear that he understood the significance of Stalin's ascent and foresaw that the party might split between the "two most talented members" of the Central Committee—Trotsky and Stalin. At the time, Trotsky himself was oblivious of all this. He did not fight for the publication of the will when Lenin died a year later. His reasons for this attitude are not certain. The will, however, was not a document that was very flattering to any of the Bolshevik leaders. Stalin was harshly criticized; Trotsky was treated with little ceremony ("administrative methods"), as was Bukharin ("no understanding of dialectics"). No one in the Politburo had a powerful motive for publishing this somber document, with its virtual premonition of disasters in the future. Lenin, architect and leader of the Bolshevik party, was thus intimately aware of what was happening within it; he showed a profound grasp of its internal situation a year before he died. Trotsky, who had little experience of party life, and had never reflected on the specific role or nature of the party, was oblivious.

After Lenin's death, Trotsky found himself alone in the Politburo. Thereafter, he made mistake after mistake. He concentrated his fire on Zinoviev and Kamenev from 1923 to 1925, and, by playing on their role in October, 1917, helped Stalin to isolate them later. Then he thought that Bukharin was his main enemy, and devoted his energies to combating him. As late as 1927, he was considering an alliance with Stalin against Bukharin. He utterly failed to see that Stalin was determined to evict him from the party, and that the only way of preventing this was a bloc of the Left and Right against the Center. Bukharin perceived this by 1927, and said to Kamenev: "There is much more that divides us from Stalin than from each other." [14] In effect, Stalin was already organizationally master of the party by 1923. Hence much of the inner-party struggle was shadowboxing. The only thing that could have defeated Stalin was political unity of the other Old Bolsheviks against him. Zinoviev, Kamenev, and Bukharin saw this too late. Trotsky, however, was prevented from ever understanding the true situation by the theoretical character

---

[14] Isaac Deutscher, *The Prophet Unarmed*, p. 442.

of his Marxism. Here, his constant underestimation of the autonomous power of political institutions, and his tendency to collapse
these back into the mass forces that were allegedly their "social
base," were his nemeses. Throughout the inner-party struggle, he
was always interpreting the political positions adopted by the
various participants as merely the visible signs of occult sociological trends within Soviet society. So Right, Center, and Left in
the party became, in Trotsky's writings, basically idealist categories, divorced from politics as such—the concrete arena of power
and institutions. Thus, in spite of Lenin's warnings about the
importance of Stalin and the alarming organizational power he
was accumulating, Trotsky persisted in seeing Kamenev and
Zinoviev as the main threat to him in the party, because they were
the ideologues of the triumvirate, who spoke in the conventional
idiom of ideas. This constant correlation—ideas: social forces—
with its lack of any intermediary theory of the political level, led
to disastrous practical mistakes in the prosecution of Trotsky's
own struggle.

A particularly obvious example of this was his publication
of the sequence of articles that make up *The New Course* (1923).
In these, he explicitly states:

> The different needs of the working class, of the peasantry, of the
> state apparatus and of its membership act upon our party, through
> whose medium they seek to find a political expression. The diffi-
> culties and contradictions inherent in our epoch, the temporary
> discord in the interests of the different layers of the proletariat,
> or of the proletariat as a whole and the peasantry, act upon the
> party through the medium of worker and peasant cells, the state
> apparatus, the student youth. *Even episodic differences in views
> and nuances of opinion may express the remote pressure of
> distinct social interests. . . .*[15]

Here the obverse side of the notion of "substitutionism" is
evident—the assumption of a possible "identity" between parties
and classes. The use of this couplet necessarily obscured the obvious fact that the relations between the two are never simplifiable
to either of these poles. In one sense, a party is always a "substitute" for a class, in that it does not coincide with it—if it did, there

---

[15] Leon Trotsky, *The New Course*, p. 27 (my italics).

would be no need for a party—and yet it acts in the name of the class. In another sense, it is never a "substitute" for it, in that it cannot abolish the objective nature of the proletariat and the global relation of class forces, which do not cease to exist even when the proletariat is dispersed and diminished, as after the Civil War, or when the party acts against the immediate interests of the working class, as it did during the New Economic Policy. The relations between party and class form a spectrum of complex, changeable possibilities that are not negotiable within these bipolar descriptions. Thus it was noticeable that the notion of "substitutionism" did not enlighten Trotsky in his conduct of the inner-party struggle, precisely in a phase when the importance of political apparatuses—the party—had increased very greatly relative to that of mass social forces (without, however, abolishing them). He was the last to see what was happening, despite his polemical construct. Indeed, since its implied opposite—"identity" —was a regulative notion for him, he was led to critical political mistakes whenever he tried to assess the relations between party and class in this phase. The *New Course* itself represents a particularly clear example of this. The credo of sociologism quoted above was accompanied by a ringing call for the proletarianization of the composition of the party, and for its rejuvenation by an influx of the young. This reliance on sociological categories, idealistically conceived, had an ironic consequence. The very policy that Trotsky advocated for the renovation of the party and its debureaucratization was implemented by Stalin with exactly the opposite results. The Lenin Levy of 1924 decisively clinched Stalin's control of the party by swamping the veteran Bolshevik cadres with a huge mass of politically unformed and manipulable workers. The proletarian composition of the party shot up. The mistake of thinking that social forces are immediately "transposable" into political organizations was, of course, unthinkable within Lenin's theory of the party. Trotsky never abandoned it, however, in these years. In 1925, he stayed aloof when the troika split apart—viewing the struggle between Stalin and Zinoviev as a vulgar dispute in which no principle was at stake. When Zinoviev and Stalin were hurling political attacks at each other by way of the respective party organizations of Leningrad and Moscow, he wrote sarcastically to Kamenev: "What is the social basis of two workers' organizations pouring abuse upon one another?" The abstentionism of this stance, of course, was suicidal. In a sense, Trotsky never fought on the political plane at all—in contrast with, for example, Zinoviev. He was not equipped to do so by his whole theoretical training. His conduct in the inner-party struggle fluctuated between an aggressive truculence (a great *dafke* in the Jewish sense) and a profound passivity (the only salvation of Russia was the chance of revolutions abroad).[16] It never attained political-tactical coherence. The result was that he continually played into the hands of Stalin. By presenting a threat with no solid institutional or political foundations, with a great array of public gestures, Trotsky provided precisely what the apparatus and Stalin, as its most outstanding representative, needed in order to turn the party into an authoritarian and bureaucratic machine. One might almost say that if Trotsky had not existed, Stalin would have had to invent him (and in a sense he was invented by Stalin).

The Ideological and Strategic Struggle

So much for the political-tactical struggle inside the Bolshevik party. It is now necessary to consider to what extent the great ideological disputes—over the strategic options before the revolution—reflected the same theoretical constellation in Trotsky's thought. It will be seen that the parallelism is, in fact, very close. This is evident in both of the main controversies of these years.

Socialism in One Country Versus Permanent Revolution. The dispute over this issue dominated the ideological debates of the twenties. Lenin had established what was undoubtedly a correct position at the time of Brest-Litovsk. He said that the Bolsheviks should always be thinking of varying possibilities, not of false certainties. It was naïve to speculate whether revolutions would or would not occur in the West, in general. Bolshevik strategy should not be based on the presumption of an occurrence

---

16 Trotsky himself frequently spoke of "revolutionary optimism" in later years. Optimism and pessimism, of course, are emotional attitudes that have little to do with Marxism. Bourgeois Weltanschauung has traditionally weltered in such categories. The adjective "revolutionary" does not make "optimism" a more profound category than the adjective "heroic" ever made "pessimism."

of a European revolution; but neither should the possibility of one be discarded. After Lenin's death, however, this dialectical position disintegrated into polarized opposites within the party. Stalin effectively wrote off the possibility of international revolutions, and made the construction of socialism in one country the exclusive task—both necessary and possible—of the Bolshevik party. Trotsky declared that the October Revolution was doomed unless international revolutions came to its aid, and predicted that these revolutions were certain to occur. The falsification of Lenin's position is evident in either case.

It may be argued that Stalin, by discounting the possibility of successful European revolutions, effectively contributed to their eventual defeat—this accusation has often been made against his policies toward Germany and Spain. There was, indeed, an element of the self-fulfilling prediction in socialism in one country. However, given this criticism—which is precisely that Stalin's policies represented a debasement of Lenin's strategy—the superiority of Stalin's perspective over Trotsky's is undeniable. It forms the whole historical-practical context in which the struggle for power discussed above unfolded. No matter how strong Stalin's position in the apparatus, it would have availed him little if his basic strategic line had been invalidated by the course of political events. It was, on the contrary, confirmed by history. In this lay Stalin's ultimate, unshakable strength in the twenties.

Trotsky's Conception. What was Trotsky's strategic conception, by contrast? What did he mean by "permanent revolution"? In his brochure of 1928 of that name, he included three quite separate notions in the same formula: the immediate continuity between democratic and socialist stages of the revolution in any given country; the permanent transformation of the socialist revolution itself, once victorious; and the inevitable linkage of the fate of the revolution in any one country with that of the world revolution everywhere. The first was to imply a generalization of his view of the October Revolution, discussed above, now proclaimed a law in all colonial countries. The second was banal and uncontroversial—no one was going to deny that the Soviet state would ceaselessly undergo change. The critical notion was the third one: the position that the survival of the Soviet revolution depended on the victory of revolutions abroad. Trotsky's arguments for this assertion, the crux on which the whole of his political position rested, are astonishingly weak. He provides, in effect, only two reasons why socialism in one country was not practicable. Both are vague in the extreme. They seem to be that Russia's entry into the world economy would render her hopelessly vulnerable to capitalist economic blockade and subversion. "The harsh curbings of the world market" are invoked, without any account of what precise impact they would have on the nascent Soviet state.[17] Secondly, Trotsky appears to argue that the U.S.S.R. was militarily indefensible, and would collapse to external invasion unless European revolutions came to its help. It is perfectly evident that neither of these arguments was justified at the time, and that both were indeed disconfirmed by actual events. Soviet foreign trade was a motor of economic development, not of regression and capitulation—a factor of progress in the rapid accumulation of the twenties and the thirties. Nor did the world bourgeoisie pounce upon the Soviet Union in unison, sending supranational armies marching on Moscow. On the contrary, intercapitalist contradictions were such that they delayed imperialist attack on the U.S.S.R. for twenty years after the Civil War. When Germany eventually invaded Russia, the Soviet state, industrialized

---

[17] In an extraordinary passage, Trotsky actually says that if socialism were possible in Russia, world revolution would be unnecessary, because Russia was so large that the successful construction of socialism in the U.S.S.R. would be equivalent to international victory for the proletariat everywhere.

> The example of a backward country, which in the course of several five-year plans was able to construct a mighty socialist society with its own forces, would mean a deathblow to world capitalism, and would reduce to a minimum, if not to zero, the costs of the world proletarian revolution.

This is, of course, precisely the view implicitly advocated by Khrushchev in the early sixties. Its use here shows how weak Trotsky's whole argument was in *Permanent Revolution* (1928). Trotsky's argument against socialism in one country was not that an authentic socialism was impossible in a society with such a low level of productive forces and cultural accumulation, but that the Soviet state could not survive external attack, whether economic or military. The quality of Soviet socialism was not the issue for him here. The quotation above shows that in debate Trotsky accepted a summary equation between socialism and Soviet economic development.

and armed under Stalin and assisted by bourgeois allies, was able to throw the aggressors back triumphantly.[18] There was thus no substance in Trotsky's thesis that socialism in one country was doomed to annihilation.

Theoretical Error

What is important to isolate here is the basic theoretical error that underlay the whole notion of permanent revolution. Trotsky, once again, proceeded from a schema of (hypostatized) mass social forces—bourgeoisie versus proletariat in alliance with the poor peasantry—in one country, to a universalization of this equation via its direct transposition onto a world scale, where the "international" bourgeoisie confronted the "international" proletariat. The simple formula "permanent revolution" effected this enormous jump. All it omitted was the *political* institution of the *nation*—that is to say, the whole formal structure of international relations and the system it constitutes. A "mere" political institution, bourgeois at that, evaporated like so much phosphorescence before a monumental class confrontation dictated inexorably by sociological laws. The refusal to respect the autonomy of the political level, which had previously produced an idealism of class action innocent of any party organization, now produced a global *Gleichschaltung*—a planetary social structure, soaring above its articulations in any concrete international system. The intermediary level party or nation—is in both cases simply omitted.

This idealism has nothing to do with Marxism. The notion of permanent revolution had no authentic content. It was an ideological concept designed to unify disparate problems within a single compass, at the cost of an accurate account of any of them. The expectation that successful revolutions were imminent in Europe was the voluntarist consequence of this monism. Trotsky failed to understand the fundamental differences between Russian and Western European social structures. For him, capi-

---

[18] Trotsky always argued that since the contradiction between capitalism and socialism was more fundamental than that between the bourgeois countries, they were bound to unite in an attack on the Soviet Union. This is a classic instance of the central confusion between the *determinant* contradiction in the long run, and the *dominant* contradiction in any given conjuncture.

talism was one and indivisible, and the agenda of revolution was one and indivisible, either side of the Vistula. This formal internationalism (reminiscent of that of Luxemburg) in fact abolished the concrete international differences between the various European countries.[19] Stalin's instinctive mistrust of the Western European proletariat, and his reliance on Russian particularism, showed a more accurate, if narrow and uncritical, awareness of the segmented nature of Europe in the twenties. Events vindicated his belief in the enduring importance of the nation as the unit demarcating one social structure from another.[20] Political agendas were not interchangeable across geographical frontiers in the Europe of Versailles. History kept different times in Paris, Rome, London, or Moscow.

Collectivization and Industrialization

The second, and subordinate, issue that dominated the ideological debates of the twenties was over economic policy in Russia itself. Here the crux of the dispute concerned agrarian policy. Lenin had laid down a general strategic line for the rural sector in the Soviet Union. He regarded collectivization as an imperative long-run policy, which only made sense, however, if it was accompanied by the production of advanced agricultural machinery and a cultural revolution among the peasantry. He

---

[19] Antonio Gramsci commented perceptively on Trotsky's internationalism some years later:

It should be considered whether Trotsky's famous theory of Permanent Revolution may not be the political reflection of the theory of the war of maneuver—in the last analysis the reflection of the general economic-cultural and social conditions in a country where the structures of national life are embryonic and loose, and cannot become "trench or fortress." In that case one might say that Trotsky, who is apparently "western" was, in fact, a cosmopolitan, that is superficially national and superficially western or European—whereas Lenin was profoundly national and profoundly European . . .

Note Sul Machiavelli, p. 67.

[20] Lucio Magri discusses this in "Valori e Limiti delle Esperienze Frontiste," *Critica Marxista* (May–June, 1965). It should be said that Stalin's later conception of the Cold War as simply the "class struggle on an international level" effectively equating states with classes, represented an opposite but identical error to Trotsky's in the twenties.

thought that economic competition between the collective and private sectors was necessary, not only to avoid antagonizing the peasantry but also to ensure that collective farming became efficient. He advocated experimentation with different forms of collective agriculture. These pilot projects were, of course, the absolute antithesis of Stalinist collectivization—in which deadlines were issued for the collectivization of given provinces and "socialist emulation" was unleashed among the party organizations of the different areas to reach their targets before their neighbors. Once again, however, with Lenin's death, his dialectical strategy disintegrated into polarized opposites. Bukharin advocated an ultraright policy of private peasant enrichment at the expense of the towns: "We shall move forward by tiny, tiny steps pulling behind us our large peasant cart." Preobrazhensky urged the exploitation of the peasantry (in the technical-economic sense) to accumulate a surplus for rapid industrialization.

These violently contradictory formulas concealed a necessary complementarity, which Lenin's policy had been precisely designed to safeguard. For the poorer the peasantry was, the less surplus it had over and beyond what it consumed itself, and the less it was "exploitable" for industrialization. Bukharin's conciliation of the peasantry and Preobrazhensky's counterposition of it to the proletariat were equally distortions of Lenin's policy, which was to collectivize but not to crush the peasantry, not to wage war on them. Both protagonists showed a vulgar Marxism that was endemic in much of the Bolshevik Old Guard. Preobrazhensky insisted that primitive socialist accumulation was an iron, inevitable "law" of Soviet society. He attacked Bukharin for Lukácsism when Bukharin claimed that economic policy in the U.S.S.R. was subject to political decision-making. Bukharin, for his part, wrote, in his *Introduction to Historical Materialism* at this time, that Marxism was comparable to a natural science, which could potentially predict future events with the precision of physics. The huge distance between formulations of this nature and Lenin's Marxism is obvious. (Lenin, of course, was the only leading Bolshevik to have studied, from the standpoint of *Capital,* Hegel, Feuerbach, and the young Marx in Switzerland during the war.)

Given this disintegration of Leninism, there is, however, no doubt that—as with the controversy over socialism in one country

—one position was superior to the other. Here, of course, it was Preobrazhensky and Trotsky who were correct in their emphasis on the need to check social differentiation in the country and bring the rural surplus under Soviet control. The imperatives of rapid industrialization were much more clearly seen, much earlier, by Trotsky and Preobrazhensky than by anyone else in the party. This was their great historical merit in these years. Trotsky's call for planned industrialization and primitive socialist accumulation dated from the Twelfth Party Congress in 1923. The bold foresight of his position contrasts with Bukharin's accommodation to retrograde economic tendencies and with Stalin's hesitations in these years. The subsequent history of the Soviet Union confirmed the comparative justice of the policies he was then advocating. What is the relation of his merits in the economic debate to his errors in the debate over socialism in one country? Is it just contingent? The answer seems to be that whereas the debate over socialism in one country concerned the international *political* articulations of the revolution, the economic debate concerned the *administrative* options of the Soviet *state*. Here Trotsky showed all his gifts as an administrator, which Lenin had noted, and his special sensitivity to the state, which has been discussed previously. His lucidity in the economic debate was thus consonant with the whole cast of his Marxism. He was supremely aware of the economic vocation of the Soviet state, at a time when the other Bolsheviks were merely preoccupied with the day-to-day problems of the New Economic Policy. However, an economic strategy for the U.S.S.R. required more than an administrative decision by the Soviet state. Its implementation required a correct *political* policy by the party toward the different social classes—what Mao was later allusively to call the "handling of contradictions among the people."

Here Trotsky had no coherent perspective to provide. His lack of grasp of party problems made this virtually inevitable. The result was that the actual implementation of his policies was enacted, and denatured, by Stalin. After defeating Trotsky and the Left, Stalin turned against the Right and put the Opposition's economic policy into practice. But he did so with a crudity and violence that precipitated a permanent agrarian crisis, despite all the tremendous gains of the Five-Year Plans. Trotsky had never concretely envisaged the problem of the political implementation of his economic policies. Stalin solved the problem with a concrete political answer—the catastrophe of forced collectivization. Trotsky, of course, recoiled from the collectivization campaigns with horror. He denounced Stalin for carrying out his policies in a manner totally contrary to his conception of them. Yet the resemblance was undeniable. This relationship was repeated on various occasions. The Lenin Levy of 1924, already discussed, was one. Later, as Deutscher comments, Stalin seems to have taken quite seriously Trotsky's constant warnings of the danger of a bourgeois restoration based on the peasantry or a bureaucratic-military coup. His way of fighting these dangers was campaigns of assassination. It seemed at these moments as if Stalin stood to Trotsky as Smerdyakov stood to Ivan Karamazov. Not just in the sense that he denatured the original inspiration when putting it into practice, but in the sense that the inspiration itself had original flaws that made this possible. We have seen what these flaws were. The fact is that, in the twenties, Leninism disappeared with Lenin. Thereafter the Bolshevik party was constantly driven from one extreme to another, by a logic of events that no leader or group had the theoretical understanding to master. Given the disintegration of Lenin's dialectical strategy, Left and Right policies bifurcated from it and yet were constantly recombined by the necessities of history itself. Thus, socialism in one country was eventually carried out with the economic program of the Left Opposition. But because this was only a combination of Left and Right policies, not a dialectical unity of strategy, the result was the crude, *ad hoc* pragmatism of Stalin and the innumerable, costly zigzags of his domestic and foreign policy. The history of the Comintern was particularly rife with these violent shifts, in which new blunders were often merely added to old blunders in the effort to overcome them. The party got through these years with Stalin's elementary political pragmatism, his ability to adapt and swerve when circumstances changed—or afterward. The fact that this pragmatism triumphed only emphasizes how steep was the drop in Bolshevik Marxism once Lenin was gone.

The tragedy of this decline was that of its historical consequences. After the Russian revolution, there was a situation in which the theoretical understanding of a small group of leaders might have meant an immeasurable difference for the whole future of the human race. Now, four decades later, we can partly perceive the fruits of the development that took place then, but the ultimate consequences are still to be seen.

1927–40

Myth

Trotsky had started his political life as a *franc-tireur,* outside the organized detachments of the revolutionary movement. During the revolution, he emerged as the great people's tribune and military organizer. In the twenties, he was the unsuccessful leader of the Opposition in Russia. After his defeat and exile, he became a myth. The last period of his life was dominated by his symbolic relationship to the great drama of the previous decade, which had become for him a tragic fate. His activities became most futile. He himself was completely ineffective—the leader of an imaginary political movement, helpless while his relatives were exterminated by Stalin, and interned wherever he went. His main objective role in these pitiful years was to provide the fictive negative center needed by Stalin in Russia. When no opposition any longer existed inside the Bolshevik party, after Stalin's purges, Trotsky kept on publishing his bulletin of the Opposition. He was the main accused at the Moscow Trials. Stalin installed his iron dictatorship by mobilizing the party apparatus against the "Trotskyite" threat. The myth of his name was such that the bourgeoisies of Western Europe were constantly afraid of it. In August, 1939, the French ambassador Coulondre said to Hitler that, in the event of a European war, Trotsky might be the ultimate victor. Hitler replied that this was a reason that France and Britain should not declare war on him.

This phase of Trotsky's life may be discussed at two levels. His efforts to forge political organizations—a Fourth International —were destined to failure. His unfamiliarity with the sociopolitical structures of the West—already evident in the debate on permanent revolution—led him to believe that the Russian experience of the first decade of the twentieth century could be duplicated in Western Europe and the U.S.A. in the thirties. This error was linked, of course, to his parallel incomprehension of the nature of a revolutionary party. In his old age, Trotsky now believed that his great mistake had been to underestimate the importance of the party, which Lenin had seen. But he had not learned from Lenin. Once again, as in his early youth, his attempt to duplicate Lenin's party construction merely led to a caricature of it. It was an external imitation of its organizational forms, without any understanding of its intrinsic nature. Uncertain of the character of the new societies in which he found himself, and unaware of the necessary relationship between party and society as Lenin theorized it, Trotsky's organizational ventures lapsed into a futile voluntarism. By a supreme irony, he often found himself, at the end of his life, in the midst of precisely those salon intellectuals—the antithesis of the Leninist revolutionary—whom he had always detested and despised. For many of them were political recruits to his cause, especially in the United States—the Burnhams, Schachtmans, and others. It was pathetic, of course, that Trotsky should have entered into serious argument with creatures such as Burnham. His very association with them was graphic evidence of how lost and disoriented he was in the unfamiliar context of the West.

Trotsky's writings in exile are, of course, of much greater importance than these ill-starred ventures. They do not add substantially to the theoretical constellation already described. But they confirm Trotsky's stature as a classical revolutionary thinker, stranded in an impossible historical impasse. His characteristic, if erratic, intuition for mass social forces is what gives his later writings their merit. The *History of the Russian Revolution* is, as has often been pointed out, above all a brilliant study in mass psychology and its complementary opposite, individual portraiture. It is not an account of the role of the Bolshevik party in the October Revolution so much as an epic of the crowds who were led to victory by it. Trotsky's sociologism here finds its most authentic and powerful expression. The idealism that it necessarily involved produces a view of the revolution that explicitly rejects political or economic variables as of permanent importance. The *psychology* of the *class,* a perfect combination of the constant couplet—social forces and ideas—becomes the determinant instance of the revolution:

In a society that is seized by revolution, classes are in conflict. It is perfectly clear, however, that the changes introduced between the beginning and the end of a revolution in the economic bases of society and its social substratum of classes are not sufficient to explain the course of the revolution itself, which can overthrow in a short interval age-old institutions, create new ones, and again overthrow them. *The dynamic of revolutionary events is directly determined by swift, intense and passionate changes in the psychology of classes* which have already formed themselves before the revolution.[21]

Trotsky's essays on German Fascism are a pathology of the class nature of the dispossessed petite bourgeoisie and their paranoias. These essays, with their tremendous prescience, stand out as the only Marxist writings of these years to predict the catastrophic consequences of Nazism and the folly of the political policies of the Third Period of the Comintern toward it. Trotsky's subsequent work (1936) on the Soviet Union itself was more serious than the demagogic title [22] under which it was published indicated. Here his lifelong sociologism was an asset.

In practical political struggle, before and after the revolution, his underestimation of the specific efficacy of political institutions led him into error after error. But when he eventually tried to confront the problem of the nature of Soviet society under Stalin, it saved him from the pitfall of judging Russia by the standards of what later became "Kremlinology." When many of his followers were manufacturing new "ruling classes" and "capitalist restorations" in the Soviet Union at will, Trotsky in his analysis of the Soviet state and party apparatus emphasized, on the contrary, that it was not a social class.

Such was Trotsky's Marxism. It forms a consistent and characteristic unity, from his early youth to his old age. Trotsky should be studied today, along with Georgy Plekhanov, Karl Kautsky, Rosa Luxemburg, Nikolai Bukharin, and Joseph Stalin, because the history of Marxism has never been reconstituted in the West. Only when it is will the stature of Lenin, the one great Marxist of that epoch, be available.

---

[21] *History of the Russian Revolution,* p. xvii (My emphasis).
[22] *The Revolution Betrayed.*

ERNEST MANDEL

"Trotsky's Marxism": An Anti-Critique

Nicolas Krassó's critique of Trotsky's political thought and activities provides a welcome occasion to unravel some of the misconceptions and prejudices about the historical role of the founder of the Red Army, which still haunt a large part of the non-engaged left intelligentsia. The roots of these misconceptions are easily discovered. The public admission and denunciation of some of Stalin's worst crimes by the present Soviet leaders are by no means accompanied by an adoption of the policies for which Trotsky fought during the last fifteen years of his life. Neither in the internal organization of the "socialist" countries, nor in their international policy (with the single exception of Cuba), have their leaders gone back to the principles of Soviet democracy and revolutionary internationalism that Trotsky defended. But historically, the very fact that Stalin has been thrown down from his pedestal, and that many accusations launched against him by Trotsky are now accepted as correct, represents a tremendous historical vindication of the man whom Stalin's agent murdered on August 20, 1940, in Coyoacan.

Anyone who remains unengaged in the struggle to bring about the final triumph of Trotsky's program—his complete political vindication—will therefore tend to rationalize his abstention by looking for faults, mistakes, and weaknesses in that program. By doing so, he cannot repeat the gross distortions and falsifications by Stalinist henchmen of the thirties, the forties, and the early fifties: that Trotsky was a counterrevolutionary and an agent of imperialism; that he wanted to, or objectively tended to, restore capitalism in the U.S.S.R. He has thus to fall back on the arguments which the more sophisticated and cleverer opponents of Trotsky advanced against him during the twenties: that he was essentially a non-Bolshevik, a left social democrat, who had not understood the peculiarities of Russia, the finesse of Lenin's theory of organization, or the complex dialectics of successful proletarian class struggle, in the West and the East. This is exactly what Krassó is doing today.

1. Classes, Parties, and the Autonomy of Political Institutions

Krassó's central thesis is quite simple: Trotsky's original sin is lack of understanding of the role of the revolutionary party, his belief that social forces can directly and immediately mold history, that they are, as it were, "transportable" into political organizations. This prevented him from ever understanding Lenin's theory of organization, and led to "sociologism" and voluntarism. From his rejection of Bolshevism in 1904, to his role in the October Revolution and in building up the Red Army, his defeat in the inner-party struggle of 1923–27, his style as a historian, and his "futile attempt" to build a Fourth International, sociologism and voluntarism constitute a single nexus. Trotsky's Marxism thus "forms a consistent and characteristic unity, from his early youth to his old age," Krassó claims.

Nobody will dispute that Trotsky rejected the essence of Lenin's theory of organization before 1917.[1] We shall not dispute

---

[1] In justice to Trotsky it must be added, however, that before 1917 Lenin likewise rejected the necessity of adopting as the strategic goal for the coming Russian revolution the establishment of the dictatorship of the proletariat. The victory of the October Revolution resulted from a historical combination of Lenin's theory and practice of the revolutionary vanguard party, and Trotsky's theory and practice of the permanent revolution.

either that the party, the ideology, and the psychology of social classes can gain a certain degree of autonomy in the historical process, or, to quote Krassó, that Marxism (not only Lenin's Marxism but any adequate interpretation of Marx's doctrine) "is defined by the notion of a complex totality, in which all the levels—economic, social, political, and ideological—are always operational, and there is a permutation of the main locus of contradictions between them." But this is a very meager basis to substantiate Krassó's thesis. When we try to analyze Trotsky's real thinking and its development through nearly forty years, we encounter at every step evidence of the incompleteness and inadequacy of Krassó's picture.

In the first place it is incorrect to say that, when rejecting Lenin's theory of organization, Trotsky borrowed his own model of a social-democratic party from the German SPD, as a "party coextensive with the working class." Historically, it would be much more correct to argue along opposite lines, i.e., to show that Lenin's theory of organization was to a large extent borrowed from the theoreticians of German and Austrian social democracy, Karl Kautsky and Viktor Adler.[2] Trotsky's mistaken opposition to Lenin's theory, at least in its rational kernel, was based upon his distrust of the Western social democratic *apparatus* as an essentially conservative one. Krassó himself admits a few pages later that Trotsky, already in 1905, was more critical of Western social democracy than Lenin. How could he then mold his party model on that social democracy?[3]

In the second place, it is completely untrue to insinuate that

---

[2] The *Hainfelder Program* of Austrian Social-Democracy states unambiguously in 1889: "Socialist consciousness is therefore something which has to be introduced from outside into the proletarian class struggle." Kautsky devoted an article in the April 17, 1901, issue of *Die Neue Zeit* ("Akademiker und Proletarier") to the problem of the relationship between revolutionary intellectuals and workers, in which he formulated most of Lenin's organizational concepts. There is no doubt, given the date of publication, that this article (one of a series of two) directly inspired Lenin's *What Is to Be Done?* (New York: International Publishers, 1943).

[3] One should add that Trotsky's instinctive distrust of dilettante intellectuals penetrating a workers' party stemmed from Marx and was entirely shared by Lenin, a point that Krassó adroitly forgets. Cf. Marx-Engels, Circular letter to Bebel, Liebknecht, Bracke, and others of September 17–18,

Trotsky continued to misunderstand or to reject Lenin's theory of organization after he had recognized that Lenin had been right on that issue, in 1917. There is no proof for this assumption. Lenin himself declared emphatically that, after Trotsky had understood that unity with the Mensheviks was impossible,[4] "there was no better Bolshevik than Trotsky." [5] All Trotsky's writings after 1917 insist on the key role of the revolutionary party in our age. At each turning point in his career, in 1923 with *Lessons of October* and *The New Course,* in 1926 with the *Platform of the Left Opposition,* in his critique of the Comintern's disastrous policies in China, Germany, Spain, and France, in the thirties in his *History of the Russian Revolution* and in his political testaments, the *Transitional Program of the Fourth International* and the so-called *Emergency Conference Manifesto,* he tirelessly stressed that the problem of building revolutionary parties is the key problem of this epoch: "The historical crisis of mankind is reduced to the crisis of the revolutionary leadership." [6] A queer way, indeed, to "forget" the role of the vanguard and to believe that social forces can directly and immediately mold history. . . .

It is true that, for Trotsky, a revolutionary vanguard was not

---

1897, in Marx-Engels, *Ausgewählte Schriften, Band II* (Moscow: Verlag für fremdsprachige Literatur, 1950), pp. 455–456, and V. I. Lenin, "One step forward, two steps back," in *Selected Works,* Vol. I (Moscow: Foreign Languages Publishing House, 1947), p. 270, wherein Lenin heaps scorn upon the "bourgeois intellectuals who fear the discipline and the organization of the proletariat." As for the "supreme irony" that Krassó discovers in the fact that Trotsky, at the end of his life, had to discuss with "salon intellectuals," which he had always detested and despised, of the Burnham-Schachtman type, Krassó forgets that Engels had to discuss with Karl Duhring and Lenin with Bulgako, who were certainly not superior to Burnham or Schachtman. It is Krassó who does not understand here the *party-building function* of such educational polemics—well understood by all the masters of Marxism.

[4] As the text of Trotsky quoted by Krassó clearly indicates, Trotsky understood that "unity with the Mensheviks was impossible" from the moment that the Menshevik conciliationary *policy* in the 1917 revolution became clear to him.

[5] Isaac Deutscher, *The Prophet Armed* (Oxford University Press, 1954), p. 259.

[6] *The Founding Conference of the Fourth International,* published by the Socialist Workers Party (New York, 1939), p. 16.

just a cleverly built and well-oiled political machine. Such an idea, born from American bourgeois politics, which, as is well known, is often undistinguishable from gangsterism, was completely alien to Lenin, Bolshevism or, for that matter, the entire international labor movement until Stalin introduced it into the practice of the Comintern. For Trotsky, as for Lenin and any Marxist tendency, a revolutionary vanguard party should be judged objectively in the first place in the light of its *avowed program and its actual policy*. If and when the best-functioning and strongest party starts to act against the interests of the revolution and the working class, a struggle has to be led to put it right. If and when its actions become consistently and for an entire epoch contrary to the interests of the proletariat, it cannot be considered a revolutionary vanguard party anymore—and then the task of building a new one immediately arises.[7]

Of course neither Lenin nor Trotsky ever *identified* a revolutionary *party* only with a correct program. Lenin explicitly stated that the correctness of a policy could prove itself in the long run only by its ability to win over a significant part of the working class—in fact, the majority.[8] But both elements are the indispensable complements out of which a revolutionary vanguard party is built. Without a correct program and policy, a party can become objectively counterrevolutionary, whatever its

---

[7] Already on November 1, 1914, Lenin wrote: "The 2nd International is dead, overcome by opportunism . . . The 3rd International has the task of organizing the forces of the proletariat for the revolutionary onslaught upon the capitalist governments." Lenin-Zinoviev, *Gegen den Strom* (Verlag der Kommunistischen Internationale, 1921), p. 6.

[8] Already in 1908, Lenin writes:

> The fundamental precondition for this success was naturally the fact that the working class, *whose elite had created social democracy,* is distinct from all other classes of capitalist society, for objective economic reasons, by its organizational capacity. Without this precondition, the organization of professional revolutionaries would be only a game, an adventure . . .

The pamphlet, *What Is to Be Done?,* underlines again and again that the organization of professional revolutionists which it proposes has a meaning only in relation with "the really revolutionary class which arises elementarily for struggle." V. I. Lenin, "Zwölf Jahre," in *Sämtliche Werke,* Vol. XII, p. 74.

mass influence in the working class may be. Without in the long run winning mass influence in the working class, revolutionists armed with the best program will degenerate into a sterile sect.

So we see, in the third place, that far from solving the problem by stating the "autonomy of political institutions" which Trotsky is said to have misunderstood, Krassó has only posed a question without furnishing an answer. For the problem is precisely that of understanding at one and the same time the autonomy of political institutions, and the *relative character* of that autonomy. After all, it was not Trotsky, but Marx and Engels who said that all history is in the last analysis the history of class struggles! [9] Political institutions are functional bodies. When they become divorced from the social forces they are supposed to serve, they very rapidly lose all efficacy and power—except when they are used by other social forces. This is precisely what happened to Stalin and his faction inside the Bolshevik party.

Krassó says that Trotsky's "constant underestimation of the autonomous power of political institutions became his nemesis." In reality, Stalin's belief in the autonomous possibilities of "power politics" became his "nemesis" because it transformed him into an unconscious tool of social forces whose very existence he did not seem to notice till the end of his life. Had Stalin been convinced, in the early twenties, that by following the course he had entered upon he would have to kill three-quarters of the Old Bolshevik upper and middle cadres, to liquidate the Comintern,[10] to introduce forced labor into the factories, and to establish one of the harshest labor codes in modern times, he would probably have recoiled in horror: after all, he was at that time a Bolshevik of some sort.

---

[9] It was precisely Marx who first discovered the law according to which all historical struggles, whether they were conducted on the political, the religious, the philosophical or any other ideological plane, are, in fact, only more or less clear expressions of the struggle between social classes, a law in virtue of which the existence of these classes, and consequently also their collisions, are in turn conditioned by the level of development of their economic situation, by their mode of production and mode of exchange . . .
Engels, Preface to the third German edition of *The 18th Brumaire of Louis Bonaparte,* in Marx-Engels, *Selected Works,* Vol. I (Moscow: Foreign Languages Publishing House, 1958), p. 245.
[10] One of the most pathetic documents of the twenties is precisely

"Pure" power politics, which Krassó seems to admire so much, degrades its actors precisely to the point that they lose all control over their own actions. The links between conscious purpose and objective consequences of these actions fade away. In opposition to this, Marxists give a premium to *conscious* action; and consciousness implies consciousness of the decisive role of social forces, and the limitations that this role inevitably imposes upon any individual's action. Krassó's lack of understanding of this dialectical interrelationship between party and class, his unawareness of the problem, is the basic weakness of his essay.

The class cannot triumph without a vanguard party. But the vanguard party is in turn a product of the class, although not only of the class. It can only play its role if it has the support of the most active part of that class.[11] In turn, without favorable objective conditions, the class can neither produce such a vanguard party, nor can the vanguard party lead the class to victory. Finally, without conscious understanding of these problems, no vanguard party will arise, even under favorable conditions, and opportunities for victory of the revolution will be irretrievably lost for a long time.

Trotsky understood this dialectical interrelationship perfectly after 1916, and applied it to a variety of concrete conditions in such a masterly fashion that it is really preposterous to state, as Krassó does, that he "failed to see the autonomous power of political institutions." Krassó himself defines Trotsky's essays on German Fascism as "the only Marxist writings of these years to predict the catastrophic consequences of Nazism and the folly of the political policies of the Third Period of the Comintern toward it." But how could Trotsky succeed in achieving such a correct

Stalin's pamphlet *Questions and Answers,* written in 1925, in which he states that a degeneration of the Party and the State are possible, "provided" that the Soviet government's foreign policy abandons proletarian internationalism, divides regions of the world into spheres of influence with imperialism, or dissolves the Comintern—eventualities that he, of course, completely rules out, but which he was to realize himself eighteen years later.

[11] In "Left-Wing Communism: An Infantile Disorder," Lenin stresses the necessity for the Communist vanguard to win the support of "the whole working class," of "the broadest masses," before it can victoriously conquer power. Selected Works, Vol. II (Moscow: Foreign Languages Publishing House, 1947), p. 573.

analysis of the evolution of German society between 1929 and 1933 without a minute examination and understanding not only of social classes and groupings but also of their parties? Are not these brilliant writings documentary proof of his capacity to provide a correct assessment of the importance of parties—above all, the parties influential in the working class? Was not his whole warning summarized in the Cassandra call: "Either the communist and social democratic *parties* will fight together against Hitler, or Hitler will crush the German working class for a long period"? Was not this call precisely based upon Trotsky's understanding of the *inability* of the working class to tackle the threat of Fascism without a coming together of these *parties*? Was not this whole analysis fitted together with an equally minute study of the evolution of bourgeois political institutions, which allowed him to discover the universal value, in our epoch, of Marx's category of Bonapartism? In the light of all these facts, what remains of Krassó's contention that Trotsky "underestimated the autonomous power of political institutions" till the end of his life?

1923–27

2. *Struggle for Power and Social Conflicts in the Soviet Union*

When studying the "struggle for power" inside the Soviet Communist Party between 1923 and 1927, Krassó is torn between two conflicting lines of thinking. On the one hand, he argues that Trotsky committed mistake after mistake because of his underestimation of the autonomy of political institutions. He refused to make a bloc with the Right against Stalin and thereby made Stalin's victory certain; for the only way to prevent that victory was to ally all the Old Bolsheviks against Stalin. On the other hand, he argues that Trotsky had no chance of winning anyway because "virtually the whole Old Guard of the Bolsheviks" united against Trotsky in 1923; "in effect, Stalin was already organizational master of the party by 1923." Surely these two lines of thinking are self-excluding. In the first case, Stalin's victory was the result of the mistakes of his opponent. In the second case, it was inevitable.

The weakness of Krassó's analysis appears clearly from the fact that *both* versions do not offer any explanation; the facts—or rather Krassó's partial misreading of them—are just taken for granted. We are not told *why,* according to the first version, not only Trotsky but all the Old Bolsheviks misread Lenin's warnings about the importance of Stalin and ganged up with him against Trotsky, instead of joining Trotsky in his fight against Stalin. We are not told *why,* according to the second version, Stalin had suddenly become master of the party as early as 1923, while Lenin was still alive. Was all this just due to his clever inner-party maneuvering, to his "capacity of persuading individuals or groups to accept the policies he advocates" or even to his "great patience"? But if this is so, then Stalin arises as a real giant among dwarfs, and even Lenin is hopelessly outmaneuvered by the crafty General Secretary. . . .

History then becomes completely incomprehensible for social science, just an arena for "power politics" in a social vacuum. The millions of victims of forced collectivization and of the Ezhov purges; the conquest of power by Hitler; the defeat in the Spanish Civil War and fifty million victims of World War II are due essentially to some genetic accident when Joseph Dzhugashvili was conceived. Here we have the ultimate result of the insistence upon an absolute autonomy of political institutions divorced from social forces, and of the refusal to view political struggles as reflecting, in the last analysis, the conflicting interests of social forces. Marx, in the Preface he wrote to the second edition of *The 18th Brumaire of Louis Bonaparte,* noted that Victor Hugo, by considering Louis Bonaparte's seizure of power as an act of force by a single individual, "aggrandizes him instead of diminishing him, by attributing to him a personal strength of initiative without precedence in history." [12] How small appear the consequences of Louis Bonaparte's seizure of power, compared to those of Joseph Stalin!

The correct method of *understanding and explaining* what happened in Russia between 1923 and 1927, or, more correctly, between 1920 and 1936, is that which Marx suggests in the above-mentioned Preface: to show "how the class struggle created the circumstances and a situation in which a mediocre person" could appear as a hero and a dictator.

---

[12] Marx-Engels, *Selected Works,* Vol. I (Moscow: Foreign Languages Publishing House, 1958), p. 244.

In that context, what is significant about Krassó's non-Marxian method is not merely the fact that he sees the inner-party struggle as "focused on the exercise of power as such," i.e., in a certain separation even from the political issues involved. It is, above all, that he completely refuses to connect the political struggle, and its expression in a struggle over certain divergent ideas and platforms, directly or indirectly with social conflicts. Here the idea of autonomy of political institutions is pushed to the point that it becomes incompatible with historical materialism as such. In fact, when Krassó reproaches Trotsky with having written that "even episodic differences in views and nuances of opinion *may* express the *remote* pressure of distinct social interests" (our emphasis), he reproaches him for being Marxist! For what this sentence states is not, as Krassó seems to assume, a possible "identity" between parties and classes, but simply the fact that parties in the last analysis represent social interests, and cannot be understood historically otherwise than as spokesmen for different social interests. This is, after all, what Marx showed in great detail in *Class Struggles in France, 1884–1850,* and in *The 18th Brumaire of Louis Bonaparte,* not to speak of his lesser works.

Small wonder that, under these conditions, Krassó does not mention even once the social grouping that makes the whole Russian history of the twenties understandable in sociohistorical terms: the bureaucracy. One should not consider it Trotsky's personal idiosyncrasy to stress and overstress the role of the bureaucracy as a social force with separate interests from those of the proletariat.[13] As early as 1871, in their writings on the Paris Commune, Marx and Engels first drew attention to the danger that a bureaucracy could dominate a proletarian state, and they enumerated a series of simple rules in order to prevent this danger.[14] The mature Karl Kautsky, in his best period, when Lenin

---

[13] Not completely separate however—in the same way as the fascist bureaucracy can never completely separate itself from monopoly capital. But in both cases the defense of common historical interests of the class (collective property in the first case, private property in the other) are combined with a thorough *political* expropriation of that same class, and even with great individual hardships for many of its members.

[14] Karl Marx, *The Civil War in France*—Fr. Engels, "Preface to *The*

Surely Lenin saw the concrete interplay between the social process—the growing political passivity of the working class and the growing strength of the bureaucracy in the state apparatus and society, accompanied by a growing bureaucratization of the party apparatus itself—and the inner-party struggle. Surely Trotsky, following the same method, understood, after a certain delay, the same interplay and acted upon that basis.[18] The tragedy was that the other leaders of the Bolshevik party failed to see in time the danger of bureaucracy, and of Stalin mounting to absolute power as representative of the Soviet bureaucracy. All of them ended by seeing the danger at some time or other, but not at the same time, and not early enough. This is the basic explanation for the apparent ease with which Stalin conquered power.

There is no doubt that Trotsky committed tactical mistakes in the struggle—which are especially apparent today to authors such as Krassó, endowed with that unique source of political intelligence called hindsight.[19] But so did Lenin, too. After all, it

---

[18] It is untrue to say, as does Krassó, that Lenin, in his Testament, "evinced no special confidence in him (Trotsky)." The Testament presents Trotsky as the most capable member of the Central Committee. It underlines, to be sure, what Lenin considers to be his weakness, but predicts also that a sharp conflict will break out between Trotsky and Stalin, and proposes to eliminate Stalin from his central organizational position. The implication is obvious.

[19] Krassó's record of these errors is inaccurate on numerous issues. He wrongly attributes the idea of "militarization of labor" to Trotsky, whereas in reality it was a collective party decision adopted at the IXth Congress of the CPSU. He alleges that Trotsky did not fight for the publication of Lenin's will; in reality, Trotsky on this point was defeated in the party leadership and did not want to break discipline, for reasons that we shall go into further on. Trotsky "utterly failed to see that Stalin was determined to evict him from the party," states Krassó. This may have been true of 1923—but at that time nobody saw this, and Stalin himself had probably no intentions of going to that extreme. But Trotsky recognized earlier than any other Bolshevik leader the gravity of the situation in the party and the state, which, combined with Stalin's specific character, would lead not only to expulsions but even to bloody repressions. Krassó writes that Trotsky did not pay any attention when the troika Stalin-Zinoviev-Kamenev broke up. He forgets to add that out of that breakup the United Left Opposition between Trotsky and Zinoviev-Kamenev was eventually formed, and that this united front was broken in 1927–28 not by Trotsky and his friends, but by the Zinovievists.

considered himself to be his pupil, formulated this danger
uncannily prophetic way, in 1898.[15] Lenin, in *State and R*
tion, and in the first Bolshevik program after the October R(
tion, underlines the seriousness of the problem.[16]

One might have expected that an author like Krassó,
considers himself a great admirer of Lenin, would have at
paid a little attention to what became Lenin's main final bat
preoccupation that in fact grew into an obsession during the
part of his life: the struggle against bureaucracy. Already in
he rejected a definition of the Soviet Union as a workers' s
and stated instead that Russia was "a workers' state with bur
cratic deformations." His apprehension and worry grew
month to month, and we can follow it graphically from articl
article, in all his last writings, till they reach the somber prem
tions of his last essay and of his Testament.[17]

Civil War in France," in Marx-Engels, *Selected Works,* Vol. I (Moscor
Foreign Languages Publishing House, 1958), pp. 483, 516–519.

[15] Karl Kautsky, *Der Ursprung des Christentums* (13th ed.; Stuttga'
Dietz, 1923), p. 499.

[16] In Lenin's speech on the Party Program, before the VIIIth Cong
of the CPSU (March 19, 1919), he returns again and again to the sub
of bureaucracy: "The lack of culture of Russia . . . debases Soviet Po
and re-creates bureaucracy . . ." "The bureaucracy camouflage themse
into communists . . ." "To fight bureaucratism till the end, till comp
victory, is only possible if the whole population participates in the
ministration of the country . . ." Lenin, *Selected Works,* Vol. II (Mosc
Foreign Languages Publishing House, 1947), pp. 447, 450.

[17] Examples: "We see this evil (bureaucratism) rise before us i
clearer, more precise and more threatening way" (April 21, 1921);
recourse to strike struggles, in a state in which political power belong
the proletariat, can be explained and justified only by the bureaucratic
formations of the proletarian state . . ." (January 17, 1922); "But if
consider Moscow—4,700 responsible communists—and if we consider
bureaucratic machine, this mountain, who is leading and who is b
led? I doubt very much that one could say that the communists are lea
that mountain. Truly, they are not leading; they are being led." (March
1922); "Bureaucracy exists in our country not only in the Soviet ins
tions but also in those of the Party." (March 2, 1923) In the third co
to his Testament, drafted on December 26, 1922, Lenin proposes
several tens of workers should enter the Central Committee, but
chosen among those who have worked in the Soviet apparatus, bec
they are already infected with the bureaucratic virus.

was Lenin who had built the party apparatus that now suddenly started to degenerate. It was Lenin who had put his personal authority behind a series of institutional and organizational measures, which greatly helped the victory of the bureaucracy, and which, as we know today—again with hindsight—could have been avoided without destroying the revolution: the rule of personal authority of the factory manager; overreliance upon material incentives; the exaggerated identification of party and state; the abolition of the remnants of Soviet parties or groupings other than the Bolshevik party, at a moment when the Civil War was over (and while these same groupings had been tolerated during the Civil War, provided they did not collude with counterrevolution); the suppression of the traditional right of the Bolshevik party members to form factions.[20]

One can say in a more general way that, after the end of the Civil War and the beginning of the New Economic Policy, Lenin exaggerated the immediate danger that would arise out of loosening of discipline in the party, and underestimated the danger that suppression of civil liberties for non-Bolshevik Soviet tendencies, and reduction of internal democracy in the Bolshevik party, might hasten the process of bureaucratization he rightly feared. The root of this mistake lay precisely in a belief that the party autonomously defended the conquests of the proletariat. A few years later Lenin understood how mistaken this belief had been—but it was already too late to nip in the bud the danger of bureaucratization of the party apparatus.

---

[20] In fairness to Lenin one must add that, while making these mistakes, he also tried to introduce a series of safeguards that were intended to put a brake upon the process of bureaucratization of state and party. The "troika" system in the factories effectively limited the authority of the managers. The rights of the trade unions were extended (on that point, Lenin was correct in his criticism of Trotsky's trade union proposals). The principle of "maximum income" for party cadres was upheld. Although factions were abolished, the right to form tendencies was consolidated and Shlyapnikov received the promise that his oppositional views would be printed in hundreds of thousands of copies. But history has shown that the more the proletariat became politically passive and the more the power of the bureaucracy became all-pervasive, the greater became its possibilities to sweep away these safeguards by a few swift strokes, as it did in the late twenties and the early thirties.

Krassó is completely mistaken when he thinks that Trotsky underestimated the autonomous power of political institutions during his critical struggle inside the party, between 1923 and 1927. The very opposite is true. His whole political strategy of that period can be understood only in the light of his understanding of the peculiar dialectical interrelationship between the objective conditions of Soviet society in social groupings in that society, and the autonomous role of the Bolshevik party *in that particular period and under these concrete conditions.*

Because Krassó does not understand this strategy, and perforce wants to explain Trotsky's attitudes in the light of his alleged original sin, he has to throw up his hands in despair and claim complete incoherence on behalf of the founder of the Left Opposition: "Trotsky had never concretely envisaged the problem of the political implementation of his economic policies" in the twenties. These economic policies, according to Krassó, were only the results of his "gifts as an administrator of the state," and not elaborated and correct political policies toward the different social forces in the U.S.S.R. Furthermore, they were divorced from his theory of the permanent revolution, which implied that socialism in one country was not practicable, because it would succumb to "subversion" through the world market and military collapse before a foreign imperialist aggression. . . . Confronted with so many historical distortions, one wonders whether the incoherence Krassó imputes to Trotsky does not exist in his own mind.

It is, in fact, incoherent to oppose Trotsky's immediate economic program for the Soviet Union to his concept of permanent revolution.[21] How is it possible that a Marxist, who gave such preponderance to ideas, and related them according to Krassó —in such an "immediate" way to social groupings, could at one and the same time struggle for the accelerated economic growth of the Soviet Union, and say that everything depended on immediate international revolution, without which the Soviet Union

---

[21] Krassó characterizes the formula "permanent revolution" as "an inept designation that indicated the lack of scientific (!) precision even in his profoundest insights." He seems to ignore that the formula was coined by Marx himself.

would collapse? Does not the second assumption make the first struggle meaningless? This is a contradiction implicit in the *falsified* version of the theory of permanent revolution, which both his Stalinist critics of past and present, and some of his foolish ultraleft pseudofollowers, never could explain away. The mystery is easily solved when the problem is posed in correct terms: all Trotsky stated in the third "law of the permanent revolution" was the fact that a fully fledged socialist society, i.e., a society without classes, commodities, money and state, could never be accomplished within the boundaries of a single state (which was more backward than the most advanced capitalist countries, at that).[22] He never for a single moment disputed the need to *start* the job of building socialism, and to achieve an increased tempo of economic growth for this purpose, precisely as long as the revolution remained isolated within a single country. It was he, after all, who had first concretely proposed a policy for increasing the tempo of industrialization.

---

[22] In a chapter of his critique of the *Draft Program of the Comintern,* Trotsky shows in great detail that Stalin and his allies deliberately confused the question of the possibility of a victory of the socialist *revolution* in one country, which implied the necessity of a *beginning* of socialist organization and construction of the economy, with the question of the *final* victory of socialism, i.e., the establishment of a fully developed socialist society (*The Third International After Lenin* [New York: Pioneer Publishers, 1936], pp. 24–40). It is interesting to note that as late as 1924, in the first Russian edition of his *Lenin and Leninism,* Stalin himself wrote: "For the final victory of socialism, for the organization of socialist production, the efforts of one country, particularly of such a peasant country as Russia, are insufficient." Interpreted confusedly by Krassó, the economic reasons given by Trotsky for the impossibility of "socialism in one country" become perfectly reasonable when one looks at them from the point of view of "final victory" and not of "beginning to build." Obviously, a fully fledged socialist economy must have a higher productivity of labor than the most developed capitalist economy; on this, even Joseph Stalin and Nikolai Bukharin agreed. Trotsky simply argued that in an essentially autarchic economy, it would be impossible to reach a higher productivity of labor than that which the imperialist countries achieve thanks to their international division of labor. He nowhere alleged that this would lead to an inevitable "subversion" of the planned economy inside the U.S.S.R. He only stated that it would be a source of violent conflicts and contradictions, which would not enable the Soviet Union to achieve a classless society. Historical experience has completely confirmed this prognosis.

But if the whole argument only concerned the abstract theoretical problem of *achieving* a final stage of socialism (as distinct from communism, characterized by the withering away of the social division of labor), why, then, all the heat of the discussion, one might ask? Did not Trotsky make a grave tactical mistake by involving himself in such a battle, which could not be understood by the overwhelming majority of the party membership?

The truth of the matter is that it was not at all Trotsky who raised the question, but Stalin and his faction. Undoubtedly, this was a "clever" tactical move, tending to isolate Trotsky and his followers from the more pragmatically minded Bolshevik cadres. But it so happens that on precisely this issue, most of the Bolshevik Old Guard, including Lenin's widow, sided with the United Left Opposition, and that Grigory Zinoviev and Lev Kamenev in particular threw themselves into a full-fledged battle. Trotsky's opposition to the theory of achieving socialism in one country thus became the basis for his closest collaboration with the Old Guard since the Civil War.

Both Stalin's reckless game with ideas and the Old Guard's resistance to it were not accidental. In the theory of achieving socialism in one country, the bureaucracy expressed its incipient consciousness of its own power, and arrogantly turned its back upon elementary Marxist-Leninist theory. It was "emancipating" itself not only from world revolution, but also from the whole theoretical heritage of Lenin and, incidentally, from any reliance upon an active and conscious working class, both inside the Soviet Union and in the world arena. By opposing this jettisoning of elementary Marxist theory, the Old Guard expressed its basic qualities. It was willing to go along with Stalin in order to "safeguard the unity of the party" and "not to upset the safety of the dictatorship of the proletariat." It was reluctant to go beyond a point where open antagonism with basic tenets of Lenin's theory became apparent. As said above, the tragedy of the twenties is in fact the tragedy of that Old Guard—that is, of Lenin's party without Lenin. But Stalin paid it the supreme homage of wholesale physical extermination, thereby clearly indicating his conviction that it was by its very nature "irrecuperable" for the somber bureaucratic dictatorship of the thirties and forties.

Where Krassó divides Trotsky's thinking in the twenties into unrelated and incoherent bits and pieces, there is in reality dialectical unity and coherence. Trotsky was convinced that Soviet society, in transition from capitalism to socialism, could not solve its problems gradually in the framework of the New Economic Policy. What he opposed was the idea of peaceful coexistence between petty commodity production and socialist industry inside the U.S.S.R., which was just the other side of that well-known coin, "peaceful coexistence" between capitalism and the workers' state in the world arena. He was convinced that sooner or later the conflicting social forces would arrive at a point of conflagration, nationally and internationally. His policy could be summarized in the formula: favor all those tendencies which, nationally and internationally, strengthen the proletariat, its numerical and qualitative strength, its self-confidence and revolutionary leadership; weaken all those tendencies which, nationally and internationally, tend to divide the working class or its capacity and will to defend itself.[23]

Looked at from that point of view, everything falls into place and there is no longer any puzzle. Trotsky favors industrialization because this is indispensable if the proletariat is to be strengthened inside Soviet society. He favors gradual collectivization of the countryside because this is indispensable for weakening the rich peasants' pressure against proletarian state power and their threat of blackmailing the city by sudden withdrawal of grain deliveries. He favors a combination of accelerated industrialization and gradual collectivization because it is necessary to create a material-technical infrastructure for collective farms in

---

[23] We believe that history has borne out the correctness of this basic conception. Even today, after a victorious war against Nazi imperialism, and after the complete liquidation of the kulaks as a class—two violent collisions that Trotsky considered inevitable from the early twenties on—the fate of the Soviet Union continues to depend upon the outcome of current and future social conflicts, nationally and internationally. In the final analysis, its fate, as well as the fate of all mankind, depends upon the capacity of the toiling masses of the United States to disarm the rulers of that country, before they reach the final stage of power-mad lunacy and, by unleashing a nuclear world war, demonstrate in practice that they accept the slogan "rather dead than red," as Hitler did under similar circumstances, in 1944–45.

the form of tractors and agricultural machinery [24]—without which collectivization becomes an adventure that could lead to famine in the cities. He favors a course toward increasing Soviet democracy, in order to stimulate the political activity and consciousness of the working class. He is in favor of abolishing unemployment and increasing real wages—for industrialization accompanied by a lowering of the standard of living of the workers would lessen and not heighten the political self-activity of the proletariat.[25] He favors a course of the Comintern that would profit from all favorable conditions to achieve proletarian victory in other countries, in order to ameliorate the international balance of forces in favor of the proletariat. A combination of all these policies would not have avoided a first trial of strength with the enemy; but it would have allowed it to take place in much more favorable conditions than it in fact did—in 1928–32 inside Russia, and in 1941–45 internationally.

Was this program "unrealistic"? No, in the sense that the *objective* conditions for its realization did exist. No unprejudiced student of history can doubt today that, had this alternative course been followed, the Soviet proletariat and people would have been spared innumerable avoidable sacrifices and hardships, and man-

---

[24] This is but one example of the fact that Stalin did *not* take over Trotsky's program, but only parts of it, without their necessary inner logic. The Opposition had struggled from 1923 on for the building of a tractor plant in Tsaritsyne. The principle was accepted. It was not acted upon before 1928. If tractors had started to be produced from 1924–25 on, and *kolkbozes* had been built up gradually, with poor peasants voluntarily joining them on the basis of a higher productivity of labor and higher peasant income in the cooperative sector as compared with the private one, the combination of industrialization and collectivization of agriculture would have led to a situation completely different from the tragedy witnessed in 1928–32, from which the Soviet Union continued to suffer till the late fifties.

[25] The Opposition proposed as alternative sources of accumulation, compared to the ruthless lowering of the standard of living of the workers and peasants as practiced by Stalin, a special tax levied upon the rich peasants only, and a radical reduction of administrative expenses, economizing one billion gold rubles annually. The goals of the first Five-Year Plan, spread over eight or ten years instead of over five years, could have been reached with much lower sacrifices in consumption by the mass of the people.

kind would have avoided, if not a world war, at least the scourge
of victorious Fascism spread all over Europe and dozens of millions of dead. Yes, in the sense that the *subjective* conditions
for its implementation did not exist. The Soviet proletariat was
passive and atomized. It viewed the program of the Left Opposition with sympathy but, at a time of exhaustion, without the
necessary militancy to fight for it. Contrary to what Krassó seems
to think, Trotsky at no time had the slightest illusion about this.

To leave the Bolshevik party immediately, to proclaim a new
(illegal) party, was to rely exclusively upon a working class that
was becoming more and more passive. To rely upon the army, to
stage a coup d'état, meant in fact to substitute one bureaucratic
apparatus for another and to condemn oneself to become a pris-
oner of the bureaucracy. All those critics of Trotsky who reproach
him for having avoided either the first or the second of these
avenues open to him do not understand the situation in terms of
basic social and political forces. The task of a proletarian revolutionary is not to "take power" by any means, under any conditions; it is to take power in order to implement a socialist program.
If "power" can be won only under conditions that drive one away
from the realization of that program, instead of bringing one
nearer to it, it is a thousand times preferable to stay in opposition. Non-Marxist admirers of abstract "power," presumably float-
ing in the air and detached from social reality, think this to be a
"weakness." Any convinced Marxist will understand this to have
been Trotsky's supreme strength and gift to history, instead of a
"flaw" in his armor.

Was Trotsky's struggle in the twenties, then, only a "pose"
for history's sake, in order to "save the program"? Let it be said
in passing that even from that point of view it would have been
completely justified. Today it should have become obvious that
the reappropriation of genuine Marxism by the new revolutionary
vanguard in the world is greatly assisted by the fact that Trotsky,
almost alone, saved the heritage and continuity of Marxism during
the "black thirties."

But, in reality, Trotsky's struggle had a more immediate purpose. The Soviet working class was passive—but its passivity was
not mechanically predetermined for a long period. Any upsurge of
the international revolution, any shift in the inner-Soviet relation-

ship of social forces, could have brought about an awakening. The immediate instrument for these shifts could only be the Comintern and the Communist Party of the Soviet Union. Trotsky fought in order to have the party act as a brake upon the process of bureaucratic degeneration, as Lenin had called upon him to do. History has shown a posteriori that the party apparatus had already been bureaucratized to the point where it acted as a motor of, not a brake on, the process of political expropriation of the proletariat. A priori, the outcome of this struggle depended upon the concrete political options of the CPSU leadership—the Old Bolsheviks. A correct shift at the correct moment could have reversed the process—not to the point of eliminating the bureaucracy altogether (this was impossible under the conditions of a backward country and capitalist environment) but to reduce its malignancy and awaken the proletariat to renewed self-confidence. Trotsky's "failure" was thus indeed the failure of the Old Guard—which understood too late the real nature of the monstrous parasite to which revolution had given birth. But this very "failure" underlines Trotsky's understanding of the intricate and complex relationship among social forces, political institutions, and ideas in the twenties.

3. Was International Extension
of the Revolution Impossible Between 1919 and 1949?

We now reach the third tier of Krassó's critique of Trotsky's Marxism, in a certain sense the decisive one, and obviously the weakest link in his chain of reasoning: his critique of Trotsky's "expectations" of international victories of the revolution after 1923.

This whole part of Krassó's essay is dominated by a strange paradox. Krassó started out by accusing Trotsky of underestimating the role of the party. But Trotsky's hope of successful revolutions in the West, Krassó now states, was based upon his failure "to understand the fundamental differences between Russian and Western European social structures." In other words, *objective conditions* made world revolution impossible, at least between the two world wars. In opposition to Trotsky's alleged "voluntarism," Krassó here defends a position of crude socioeconomic determinism: as revolutions have not won (yet) in the West, this proves that they could not have been victorious, and if they could not have been victorious it was because of the "specific social structure" of the West. The role of the party, of the vanguard, of the leadership, the "autonomy of political institutions," is now completely eliminated from the picture—by Krassó himself, and in polemics *against* Trotsky. A strange somersault indeed. . . .

But what about Lenin? How does Krassó account for the fact that Lenin, who, to quote Krassó, "theorized the necessary relationship between party and society," was as fervently convinced as Trotsky of the necessity of building communist parties and a Communist International? Does Krassó consider this "futile voluntarism" on Lenin's behalf? How does he explain the fact that, years after Brest-Litovsk (Krassó here commits a historical distortion by earlier insinuating the contrary), Lenin continued to think that an international extension of the revolution to the West and the East was unavoidable? [26]

Krassó can only try and construct a difference between Lenin's and Trotsky's position on the dialectical interrelationship between the October Revolution and the international revolution, by attributing to Trotsky three mechanistic and childish ideas: the idea that revolutions were "imminent" in Europe; that capitalist conditions were everywhere, at least in Europe, equally ripe for revolution without any difference between specific nations; and that the victory of these revolutions was "certain." Needless to say, Krassó will find it impossible to substantiate any of these allegations. It is easy to find overwhelming documentary proof of the contrary.

---

[26] Just two quotations: "The first Bolshevik revolution has pulled the first hundred million human beings on earth out of the grip of imperialist war, the grip of the imperialist world. The coming revolutions will pull all mankind out of the grip of these wars and that world." (October 14, 1921) "You have to learn in a special sense, in order to really understand the organization, the building, the method and the content of revolutionary work. If this happens, then I'm convinced that the perspectives of world revolution will not only be good but excellent." (November 15, 1922) (Lenin, *Sämtliche Werke,* Band 33 [Berlin: Dietz Verlag, 1966], pp. 37, 418.)

As early as the Third Congress of the Comintern (1921), Trotsky, together with Lenin (both were "at the right wing" of that Congress), stated unmistakably that, after the first wave of postwar revolutionary struggles, capitalism had now gained a breathing spell in Europe. What was on the agenda was not "immediate revolution," but the preparation of the communist parties for *future* revolution, i.e., a correct policy to win the majority of the working class and create a cadre and leadership capable of leading these parties to victory when new revolutionary situations occurred.[27] Criticizing Bukharin's and Stalin's Draft Program of the Communist International, Trotsky stated explicitly in 1928:

> The revolutionary character of the epoch is not that it permits the accomplishment of the revolution, that is, the seizure of power, at every given moment. Its revolutionary character consists in profound and sharp fluctuations and abrupt and frequent transitions from an immediately revolutionary situation, that is, such as enables the Communist Party to strive for power, to a victory of the fascist or semifascist counterrevolution, and from the latter to a provisional regime of the golden mean (the Left bloc, the inclusion of social democracy into the coalition, the passage of power to the party of MacDonald, and so forth), immediately thereafter forcing the antagonism to a crisis again and acutely raising the question of power.[28]

In his final writings, he again and again characterizes our epoch as a swift succession of revolutions, counterrevolutions, and "temporary stabilizations," a succession which precisely creates the *objective conditions* for building a revolutionary vanguard party of the Lenin type.

Here indeed is the nub of the question, which Krassó does not even pose and obviously cannot answer for that reason. What is the basic assumption that is at the bottom of Lenin's organizational concepts? As Georg Lukács so aptly characterized it, it is the assumption of the *actuality of the revolution,*[29] i.e., the con-

---

[27] A typical example of "underestimation of the autonomy of political institutions," no doubt.

[28] Leon Trotsky, *The Third International After Lenin* (New York: Pioneer Publishers, 1936), pp. 81–82.

[29] Georg Lukács, *Lénine* (Paris: E.D.I., 1965), pp. 28–29.

scious and deliberate preparation for conquest of power by the proletariat when revolutionary situations occur, and the profound conviction that, given the objective laws of motion of Russian society, such revolutionary situations *had* to occur sooner or later. When Lenin wrote his book on *Imperialism,* under the influence of Rudolph Hilferding's *Finanzkapital,*[30] and when he drew up a balance sheet of the significance of World War I, he correctly extended the notion of actuality of the revolution to the entire imperialist world system: the weakest links would break first; but precisely because they were links of one chain, the entire chain would be broken up progressively.[31] This was his justification for calling for the formation of a Third International. This was the programmatic foundation of the Comintern.

Now this is a central concept with which you cannot dally frivolously. Either it is theoretically correct and confirmed by history—and in that case not only is the "third law of permanent revolution" adequate, but the main responsibility for the working-class defeats of the twenties, thirties, and early forties can then be put squarely at the door of inadequate leadership. Or Lenin's central concept after August 4, 1914, was incorrect, and experience has shown that objective conditions were not ripe for the periodic arising of revolutionary situations in the rest of Europe—and in that case it is not only Trotsky's "third law of permanent revolution" that was a "theoretical error" (to quote Krassó), but all of Lenin's endeavors to build communist parties, organized with the purpose of leading the proletariat to the conquest of power, then stand condemned as criminal

---

[30] Rudolf Hilferding, *Das Finanzkapital* (Verlag der Wiener Volksbuchhandlung) ends on p. 477 with a final paragraph characterizing finance capital as the accomplished dictatorship of Big Business, and predicts a "formidable collision of antagonistic (social) interests," which will finally transform this dictatorship of Big Business into the dictatorship of the proletariat.

[31] The pamphlet, *The Collapse of the IInd International,* written by Lenin in 1915 (Lenin-Zinoviev, *Gegen den Strom,* pp. 129–170), is centered on the idea that a revolutionary situation is developing in Europe, and that revolutionary socialists have to act in order to stimulate the revolutionary sentiments and actions of the masses. His contributions to the first two Congresses of the Communist International extend this analysis to all colonial and semicolonial countries.

splitting. Is not this, after all, what social democrats have been claiming for more than fifty years, with the same basic argument about "sociopolitical conditions" in the West being "unripe" for revolution, and Lenin "failing to understand the fundamental differences between Russian and Western European social structures"?

The balance sheet can be drawn up very quickly, at least on the level of historical experiences. Leaving aside minor countries, there was a revolutionary situation in Germany in 1918–19, in 1920, and in 1923, and a great possibility of turning a successful defense against the threat of Nazism into a new revolutionary situation in the early thirties; there was a revolutionary situation in Spain in 1931, 1934 and 1936–37; there was a revolutionary situation in Italy in 1920, in 1945, and in 1948 (at the moment of the attempted murder of Palmiro Togliatti); there was a revolutionary situation in France in 1936 and in 1944–47. Even in Britain, there was something called a general strike in the mid-twenties. Ample literature, including writings of noncommunist and nonrevolutionary sources, attests to the fact that in all these situations the unwillingness of the masses to tolerate the survival of the capitalist system, and their instinctive drive to take society's fate in their own hands, coincided with wide confusion, division, if not near-paralysis among the ruling classes—Lenin's definition of a classical revolutionary situation. If we extend the picture to the whole world, with the Chinese revolution of the twenties and the Vietnamese uprising of the early thirties blending at the end of World War II into two powerful revolutions that stimulated a worldwide revolutionary movement of the colonial and semicolonial countries, then, surely, the definition of this half-century as "the age of permanent revolution," which Isaac Deutscher and George Novack chose as the title for a paperback selection of Trotsky's writings,[32] is an adequate summary of historical experience.

Krassó now comes to the most extraordinary statement of his essay: the defeats of the European revolution in the twenties, thirties, and early forties prove that "the superiority of Stalin's perspective over Trotsky's is undeniable." Because, you see,

---

[32] New York: Dell Publishing Co., Laurel Edition, 1964.

Trotsky foresaw victorious revolutions, while Stalin "discounted the possibility of successful European revolutions." But wasn't it precisely the opposite? Trotsky did not believe at all in automatically victorious revolutions—neither in Europe, nor anywhere else. He only tirelessly fought for a *correct policy* of the communist movement, which would enable it eventually—if not the first time, then the second, or the third one—to transform revolutionary situations into revolutionary victories. By advocating *incorrect policies,* Stalin contributed heavily to the defeats of these revolutions. He taught the Chinese Communists to put their trust in Chiang Kai-shek and, in a public speech held on the very eve of Chiang's wholesale massacre of the Shanghai workers, expressed his firm belief in the executioner as a "faithful ally." [33] He taught the German Communists that social democracy was their main enemy, and that Hitler would either be unable to conquer power or would be unable to stay in power more than a few months: they would be the real victors very soon. He taught the Spanish Communists to stop their revolution and to "first win the war," in alliance with the "liberal" bourgeoisie. He taught the French and Italian Communists to build a "new democracy" that would not be any more "entirely" bourgeois because of a few communist cabinet ministers and a few nationalizations.

All these policies ended in disaster. Yet when Krassó draws up the balance sheet of the disasters, he concludes . . . that Stalin's perspective was undeniably (!) superior to Trotsky's, for, you see, he "discounted the possibilities of successful European revolutions"! Perhaps the Stalin course of the Third International, the transformation of the Comintern from a tool of world revolution into a simple aid to diplomatic maneuvers of the Soviet government, and the theory of achieving the building of socialism in a single country, had something to do with the absence of successful European revolutions? Or would Krassó go so far as

---

[33] It is in deliberate travesty of historical truth that the Maoist leadership of the Chinese Communist Party continues to make the leader of the CCP of the 1925-27 period, Chen Tu-hsiu, mainly responsible for these mistakes, and hides the fact that he was only acting upon the direct and pressing instructions of the Communist International, and in the first place of Stalin personally.

to impute to Stalin the intention of deliberately organizing these defeats . . . just to "prove" the "superiority" of his perspectives over those of Trotsky?

As Marxists, we have to pose a final question. Stalin's "mistakes" in the realm of the Communist International cannot be explained away as accidental results of his "lack of understanding" or "Russian provincialism," any more than the disastrous results of his policies inside the Soviet Union can be explained by the thoroughly un-Marxist formula of the "personality cult." [34] His "mistaken" tactics in no way corresponded to the interests of the Soviet or the international proletariat. They cost millions of deaths which could have been saved, decades of avoidable sacrifices, and years of terrible sufferings under the iron rule of Fascism. How, then, can one explain the fact that Stalin systematically opposed or sabotaged all attempts by communist parties to take power, outside of the realm of the Soviet army, anywhere in the world, for nearly thirty years? [35] Surely, a *social* explanation must be found for this astonishing fact. Such a systematic policy can only be explained as the expression of the *particular interests of a special social grouping* inside the Soviet society: the Soviet bureaucracy.

This grouping is not a new class. It does not play a particu-

---

[34] But wasn't Stalin's policy vindicated by the U.S.S.R.'s victory in World War II, ask many people, and as Krassó also insinuates? To see things like this—completely passing over in silence the tremendous price paid for that victory, and the innumerable avoidable victims and defeats (including during the war: a whole literature has sprung up on the Soviet Union around this theme!)—is to present a distorted picture of reality. A man on the fifth floor refuses to take the elevator or even to switch on the light, but wants perforce to descend a narrow staircase in the dark. He slips, as could be expected, falls down the stairs, but thanks to his robust constitution does not break his neck, but only both arms and legs, and is even able to walk on crutches again after four years. This is obviously proof of a strong constitution; but does it argue against taking the elevator?

[35] As we know today, Stalin also tried to influence the Yugoslav and Chinese Communists against conquering power. He instructed the Vietnamese CP to stay inside the French colonial empire, rechristened the "French Union." The party he had educated obstinately refused to engage upon Fidel Castro's road toward a victorious socialist revolution in Cuba for several years. Don't these facts need a *sociological* and not a simply *psychological* explanation?

lar and objectively necessary role in the process of production. It is a privileged outgrowth of the proletariat after its conquest of power under objective conditions unfavorable for the blossoming of socialist democracy. Like the proletariat, it is fundamentally attached to collective ownership of the means of production and opposed to capitalism: that is why Stalin finally crushed the kulaks and stood up against the Nazi invasion. It has not destroyed the basic socioeconomic conquests of the October Revolution; on the contrary, it has conserved them, be it by means that enter more and more into conflict with the basic goals of socialism. The socialized mode of production born of the October Revolution has withstood successfully all assaults from outside and all undermining from within. It has proved its superiority to hundreds of millions of human beings. This is the *basic* historical trend which, incidentally, also explains why world revolution, instead of being definitively thrown back for decades as pessimists assumed, could so easily rise again and conquer momentous victories after World War II.

But unlike the proletariat, it is basically conservative in outlook, afraid of any new upsurge of world revolution, because it feels that this would trigger a new stage of workers' militancy inside its own country, which would threaten its own power and privileges. The theory and practice of "socialism in one country" in the twenties and thirties, like the theory and practice of "peaceful coexistence" in the fifties and sixties, are a perfect expression of the socially contradictory nature of that bureaucracy. It will certainly defend itself when threatened with extinction by imperialism; it will even try to extend its "zone of influence" when this can be done without upsetting the social equilibrium of forces on a world scale. But it is basically attached to the status quo. American statesmen have found this out, in the long run. Krassó should show at least their awareness of this rationale of Russian foreign policy since Lenin's death, and he should try to find a social explanation for this consistent behavior. He will find no other than the one that Trotsky elaborated.

The bureaucracy and its apologists can, of course, try and rationalize that policy, stating that it was merely concerned with the defense of the Soviet Union against the threat of all capitalists ganging up against it, if "provoked" by revolutions elsewhere. In the same way social democrats have consistently argued that they oppose revolutions only in order to defend the working-class organizations and conquests, which would be crushed by reaction if the bourgeoisie was "provoked" by revolutionary activity. But Marx taught us precisely not to judge parties and social groups on the basis of their self-rationalizations and self-proclaimed intentions, but on the basis of their objective role in society and the objective results of their actions. In that sense, the true social nature of the Soviet bureaucracy is reflected in the sum total of its actions, in the same way that, according to Lenin, the true social nature of the trade-union bureaucracy and the petit-bourgeois top echelons of social democracy in the imperialist countries *explains* their consistent opposition to socialist revolution.

Here we are again at our starting point. Marxists understand the relative autonomy of political institutions, but this understanding implies a constant research into the social roots of these institutions and into the social interests that they serve in the last analysis. It also implies that the more these institutions rise above the social classes that they first were said to serve, the more they succumb, independently of their own will, to a tendency toward self-defense and self-perpetuation, and the more they can enter into conflict with the historical interests of the class from which they arose. This is the way Marx and Lenin understood the problem. In this sense, Krassó's charge that Trotsky "underestimated" the possibility of autonomy of "parties" and "nations" is just an accusation that he was a Marxist and a Leninist. We are sure that Trotsky would have been willing to carry the cross of that sin with stoicism and not without satisfaction.

NICOLAS KRASSÓ

Reply to Ernest Mandel

Ernest Mandel's reply to my critique of "Trotsky's Marxism" requires some comment. It may be most rewarding to consider the three fundamental questions he raises, and to focus discussion on these. Most of the local issues at dispute will be resolved in so doing. The whole aim of my analysis was to try and reconstruct the *unity* of Trotsky's thought and practice as a Marxist: its singular character and coherence. Mandel's reply renounces any attempt to seek such a unity. Chronologically, he separates the Trotsky of 1904 from that of 1905 and that of 1912 from that of 1917; the Trotsky of 1926 is dissociated from that of 1922. Structurally, Trotsky's thought is divorced from his practice as a politician. My purpose was to show that the *differentia specifica* of Trotsky's activity taken as a whole may not simply be identified with abstract principles. Mandel makes virtually no reference throughout to Trotsky's style of leadership within the party, his role as a military commander, or his record as a state administrator. It is thus important to emphasize, at the outset, that Mandel has provided selective criticisms of the theses of the original essay. He has not provided a countertheory of Trotsky's Marxism. By opting for this course, he has run the risk of empiricism. A corollary of this is a recurring tendency to revert to the traditional

Trotsky-Stalin comparison, from the impasse of which it was one of the purposes of the essay to free debate. The struggle between Trotsky and Stalin in the twenties is often seen as a struggle between principles. Yet the Trotsky-Stalin polarization was a disaster, as Lenin in his will had predicted it would be. Today, the necessary point of departure to assess Trotsky *and* Stalin is Lenin. This is the axiom that governed the course of the whole argument. By dividing Trotsky's thought into discrete episodes, separating it from his practice, and relating it to an abstract antipode, Mandel has prevented himself from situating Trotsky properly within history or Marxism.

1. Trotsky and the Party

Mandel denies that Trotsky showed a consistent sociologism and a constant underestimation of the autonomous role of political institutions. The initial period of Trotsky's career—1902–17—is crucial here. Mandel's argument is twofold. He denies that Trotsky's model of the revolutionary party was derived from the German SPD—the idea of a party coextensive with the working class, as opposed to Lenin's model in *What Is to Be Done?* (in *Selected Works* [New York: International Publishers, 1943]). Yet the only occasion on which he wrote on the party as such was in his virulent attack on Lenin of 1904 (*Nashi Politicheskie Zadachi*). Deutscher explicitly comments: "To this conception of a party acting as a *locum tenens* for the proletariat [i.e., Trotsky's caricature of Lenin's conception—N. K.], he opposed Axelrod's plan for a "broadly based party" modeled on European social democratic parties." [1] The same pamphlet was prolific in encomia of the Menshevik leaders, the main protagonists of such a model for Russia. Two years later, in 1906, writing *Results and Prospects,* Trotsky expressed the greatest suspicion of the Western social democratic parties; yet this did not lead him to revise his notion of the revolutionary party, but to forget the concept altogether. The result was the unmediated reliance on mass forces, the

---

[1] Isaac Deutscher, *The Prophet Armed* (Oxford University Press, 1954), p. 90.

"social-revolutionary fatalism" that he himself later confessed.[2]

Mandel, however, claims that it was Lenin, not Trotsky, who to a large extent borrowed from the theoreticians of German and Austrian social democracy in his theory of party organization. Such a statement is astonishing when one considers that the whole emphasis of Lenin's theory was on the creation of a party of *professional revolutionaries* dedicated to making the revolution, a notion anathema to Karl Kautsky and Viktor Adler. What else was the historic split with the Mensheviks based upon? It is no accident that Trotsky was quite unable to comprehend the significance of this at the time. There is no evidence that at any stage thereafter Trotsky genuinely learned the lesson of Lenin's theory of the party. In 1917, he rallied decisively to the Bolsheviks and played a commanding role during the October Revolution. But Mandel himself involuntarily shows the continuing limitation of his political thought when he says: "Trotsky understood that unity with the Mensheviks was impossible from the moment that the Mensheviks' conciliatory *policy* [his italics] in the 1917 Revolution became clear to him." [3] Precisely. Trotsky rallied to Lenin, not because of his *organizational theory of the party*, which was the necessary historical rationale of his split with the Mensheviks, but because of his insurrectional policy of 1917. No one should underestimate the importance of this conversion. But it was just the difference between these two that created the persistent doubt and mistrust of Trotsky within the Bolshevik party after the October Revolution.

The whole subsequent history of the inner-party struggle is quite incomprehensible unless this fundamental fact is assimilated. Mandel nowhere confronts the issue. His only reference to it is a quote from Lenin to the effect that after 1917 "there was no better Bolshevik than Trotsky." It so happens, however, that this "quotation" is mere hearsay, as Isaac Deutscher (whom Mandel cites for his source) makes clear.[4] There is no firm evidence that Lenin ever made such a statement in conversation. There is evidence, however, of a negative nature: the fact is that in all the

---

[2] *Permanent Revolution* (1928), p. 49.
[3] *New Left Review,* 47, p. 34.
[4] *The Prophet Armed,* p. 259.

voluminous writings of Lenin after 1917, he never commented on Trotsky's Marxism or on the character of his conversion to Bolshevism. This silence, when he had so many opportunities of getting the record straight, is surely curious. His laconic comment on Trotsky in his will is the only secure judgment that we have.

During the thirties, of course, Trotsky did indeed give tremendous emphasis to the role of the party in the making of history. But, as I pointed out, this emphasis, which took the form of attempting to launch a Fourth International, only reflected his inability to achieve a genuine appropriation of Lenin's theory. But the consciousness of past error tended to produce new ones. Trotsky never deeply studied or experienced Lenin's theory of the party or its relation to society. When he tried to reproduce it in the thirties, he caricatured it—giving it a voluntarist and idealist twist consonant with the whole previous character of his Marxism, but remote from Lenin's. Thus, in the very sentence that Mandel quotes, he could write: "The historical crisis of mankind *is reduced* to the crisis of the revolutionary leadership." [5] The colossal social, economic, and political blockages of world history in the thirties are "reduced" to a question of "leadership." Such an idealist formulation is surely incompatible with Lenin's mode of thought: the subjectivism and monism are evident. A corollary of the notion of leadership here is the fetishization of the *program* in Trotsky's later thought. This becomes the sovereign instance of revolutionary efficacy—fundamentally dissociated from the structure of the *party,* which was the anchor of Lenin's thought. The program thus conceived becomes an idealist *virtu* above politics, where Lenin's insistence on organization, by contrast, related it permanently to the social structure and to the objective contradictions at work within it. Hence the enormous difference in practical outcomes of the two experiences of "party-building." The one was locked to the deepest internal movement of Russian society of its time. The other never achieved any purchase in the West. At the end of his life, Trotsky remembered the Lenin he had ignored at the beginning of it. He never succeeded in retracing him.

---

[5] *New Left Review*, 47, p. 35.

2. The Struggle of the Twenties

The concrete course of the inner-party struggle is only intelligible in the light of Trotsky's non-Leninist past. For it was this that both isolated him from the Old Guard and led him to numerous tactical miscalculations within the party. The objective and subjective results of his long absence from inner-party life were decisive here. Mandel argues that it is contradictory to state that Trotsky made error after error in his fight against Stalin *and* that Stalin was already organizationally master of the party of 1923. "Surely these two lines of thinking are self-excluding? In the first case, Stalin's victory was the result of the mistakes of his opponent. In the second case, it was inevitable." [6] In fact, the argument was that *organizationally* Stalin was master of the party in 1923, but that *political* unity of the Old Guard against him was the one force that could have defeated him. The organizational master of the party was not already the absolute ruler of the country. Stalin, presenting himself as the representative of collective leadership, could have been successfully challenged by a genuine collective leadership. An alliance of Nikolai Bukharin, Leon Trotsky, Grigory Zinoviev, and Leo Kamenev in 1923 would doubtless have prevailed. [7] This dialectical formulation defines the central issue: *why* did that political unity never occur? Mandel implicitly admits that this is the correct question to ask, but he himself poses it in a despairing and agnostic manner:

> The tragedy was that the other leaders of the Bolshevik party failed to see in time the danger of bureaucracy, and of Stalin mounting to absolute power as the representative of the Soviet bureaucracy. All of them ended by seeing the danger at some time or other, but not at the same time, and not early enough.

---

[6] *Ibid.*, p. 37.

[7] In my first essay, I pointed out the objective complementarity of left and right policies—a central thesis Mandel ignores. The problem confronting the party was the form the synthesis would take. In fact, the left-right unity that leftists and rightists did not achieve was fostered by Stalin in three forms. First, by the elementary amalgam of rightism and leftism in the zigzags of official Soviet policy. Second, by giving birth to the myth that such an antiparty block actually existed. Third, by accomplishing the unity of leftists and rightists in the prisons.

This is the basic explanation for the apparent ease with which Stalin conquered power.[8]

It is *this* formulation which provides no explanation whatever for the fact that it concedes. Accident or aberration are the only causal factors possible, once it is merely a question of the other Bolshevik leaders "not seeing in time" the danger of Stalin's ascent to power. By contrast, my own account renders the division of the Old Guard immediately explicable. Trotsky was viewed, not as an ally but as the main *threat,* by the other Bolshevik leaders because of his non-Leninist past, because of his military supremacy, because of his authoritarian role during War Communism, and because of his commandism in the trade union debates. Bonapartism was not, as Mandel implies, a Marxist category rediscovered by Trotsky during the thirties: [9] it was the very danger that Bukharin, Zinoviev, and the others saw in Trotsky. At the same time, the very lack of party experience that provoked these suspicions of Trotsky was what prevented him from understanding and overcoming them. He was by and large lost in factional combat, which he always tended to interpret as the ideological transposition of sociological conflicts in society as a whole. Hence he saw Zinoviev, and then Bukharin, as his main enemy, because they were the "ideologues" of the dominant coalition at different times: a symmetrical error. Trotsky became the leader of an opposition who was himself unaware for a long time that his main opponent was Stalin. The result was that he actually tended to unite the party against himself. The fear of a paper tiger made the party functionaries breed a real tiger; they learned this a decade later. In the twenties, Trotsky as a negative center accelerated the authoritarian and bureaucratic tendencies in the party. The "primitive accumulation" of Stalin's power was born from the self-defense of the Old Guard against Trotsky. For Trotsky, the Old Guard was timorously yielding to the social pressure of retrograde Russia. For the functionaries of the party, Trotsky was a dangerous adventurist. Hence Trotsky's drive to divide the party along lines of pure "principles" ironically created an "unprincipled" alliance against him. Stalin won allegiance for his realism because the party machinery was very conscious of its

---

8 *Ibid.,* p. 40.
9 *Ibid.,* p. 37.

isolation from the masses. Stalin was neither a rightist nor a leftist, and the men of the apparatus instinctively felt that he was not a centrist either. For them, he represented an elementary, single-minded idea that had a tremendous appeal: power must be kept. Stalin's relative necessity was the *vis inertiae* of the situation. It was the path of least resistance for keeping power and developing in a noncapitalist fashion. Stalin thus became identified with the substance of power, even for his opponents. Bukharin said to Kamenev in 1928: "Is not our situation hopeless? If the country perishes, we perish with it (i.e., the party). If the country manages to recover, and Stalin changes course in time, we still perish." [10] Trotsky never understood this complex. The result was a sequence of political blunders, documented in my essay, which ensured the victory of Stalin.

The critical importance of the problem of the Old Guard was a product of the sociopolitical context of Russia at the time. For the political institution of the party existed in a virtual social vacuum after the Civil War. This is what accounts for the decisive character of Trotsky's mistakes within the party, which were the natural expression of his general underestimation of the autonomy of political institutions. Sociologism is always a theoretical error; but it was especially disastrous in the Russia of the twenties, for the dialectic of mass social forces had temporarily been crippled in the Civil War. The disintegration of the working class virtually excluded it, as a deliberate actor, from the political process. After Kronstadt, nobody dared to think of an appeal to the masses (such as Mao was to make in China during the sixties, in a very different historical situation). Thus the fate of socialism was suddenly thrown onto the summit of the revolution, while its base was eroded. Trotsky's basic misunderstanding of this situation may be seen in Mandel's contradictory account of his general perspective during the twenties. On the one hand, Mandel says that Trotsky's political program was "unrealistic" because

> the *subjective* (his italics) conditions for its implementation did not exist. The Soviet proletariat was passive and atomized. It viewed the program of the Left Opposition with sympathy but, at a time of exhaustion, without the necessary militancy to fight

---

10 Isaac Deutscher, *The Prophet Armed*, p. 450.

for it. Contrary to what Krassó seems to think, Trotsky at no time had the slightest illusion about this.[11]

But the next moment, Mandel says the opposite. Trotsky's struggle was not just a matter of honor to "save the program," in lucid awareness of inevitable defeat.

> The Soviet working class was passive—but its passiveness was not predetermined mechanically for a long period. Any upsurge of the international revolution, any shift in the inner-Soviet relationship of social forces, could have brought about an awakening. The immediate instrument for these shifts could only be the Comintern and the Communist Party of the Soviet Union.[12]

These two claims are irreconcilable. They merely indicate the difficulty for any *ex post facto* justification of Trotsky's course. The truth is that Trotsky did not believe that his program was "unrealistic." His dispute with Khristian Rakovsky in 1928 makes this absolutely clear, for Rakovsky did believe exactly this. His "Letter to Valentinov" stands out as perhaps the most clairvoyant social analysis of the decade: Trotsky emphatically rejected it. The reason he did so is, of course, that he believed in the immediate fighting potential of the Soviet proletariat; this was, indeed, the assumption of his whole conduct in the inner-party struggle. What he critically underestimated was the degree of disintegration of the working class after the Civil War. Lenin, once again, was by contrast acutely aware of this. His formulation of the problem was characteristically radical: "Where is your large-scale industry? Why is it idle?" he asked in 1921. This was the nub of the problem: not the "passivity" of the proletariat (Mandel's phrase)—a subjective, conjunctural state, but its disintegration and dispersal—an objective, structural condition. Its numbers were reduced by two-thirds, and its composition was transformed, with its best militants dead or transferred to party functions. This is the sociological background of the inner-party struggle, and one which Lenin at the start of the decade—and Rakovsky at the end of it—perceived. Trotsky, believing in the immediate predominance of social forces, did not.

Does this mean that the CPSU was a political entity completely divorced from the objective social structure of Soviet Rus-

---

[11] *New Left Review,* 47, p. 45.
[12] *Ibid.,* p. 45.

sia? Of course not. Marx's thought founded *both* the autonomy of the political instance within the complex social totality, *and* its determination in the long run by the economy. The opposite mistake to that of Trotsky is any belief in the all-powerful role of political institutions as such, abstracted from the socioeconomic formation into which they are always necessarily articulated.[13] Mandel provides an excellent definition of the consequences of any such belief, when he writes:

> Pure power politics degrades its actors precisely to the point where they lose all control over their own actions. The links between conscious purposes and objective consequences of these actions fade away. In opposition to this, Marxists give a premium to *conscious* action; and consciousness implies consciousness of the decisive role of social forces, and the limitations that this role inevitably imposes upon any individual's action. . . . Stalin's belief in the autonomous possibilities of "power politics" became his "nemesis" because it transformed him into an unconscious tool of social forces whose very existence he did not seem to notice till the end of his life.[14]

There is the germ of a new and scientific account of Stalin's historical role here, free of the personalization which disciples and foes alike have pursued.[15] Such an account would have to establish a meaningful relation between his effortless victory within the party in the twenties and his ferocious purges of it during the thirties. For Stalin certainly feared the consolidation of a new social group within the party and state apparatus, and he did not hesitate to decimate his own following when he became aware of the danger (somewhat before the end of his life). As I pointed

---

13 It is odd that I should be accused of reducing everything to a power struggle within an organizational framework. I do not admire power politics. Even politics in a wider meaning of the word, although it has a relative structural autonomy, is always more than mere politics. For the socialist revolutionary, consciously so.

14 *New Left Review*, 47, p. 36.

15 It is incorrect for Mandel to imply that Stalin was a mediocre person comparable with Napoleon III. Neither was he a "giant among dwarfs." His personal characteristics were, of course, a necessary condition of his historical role, but it was the political context that determined their impact. It is possible that the negative characteristics of Trotsky were more significant than the positive characteristics of Stalin—the *übergreifendes Moment*—in the genesis of Stalin's ascendancy.

out, it was as if he took Trotsky's warnings of a "bureaucratic restoration" with deadly seriousness in the thirties.[16]

What is important to emphasize here is that the problem of bureaucratism was, as Mandel states, a central concern to Lenin in his last years. In the twenties, the temporary stabilization of capitalism had become a fact. Lenin constantly repeated, with greater and greater emphasis, that revolutionary politics had to unite fundamental intransigence with the ability to make compromises. As early as 1918, Lenin wrote, in his article "The Principal Task of Our Day—Left-Wing Infantilism and Petit Bourgeois Mentality," of the Russian weakness that "we have neither a high degree of culture nor the habit of compromise." [17]

It is obvious that the less a politician is willing to compromise with the reality of a situation, the less he is able to contribute to its solution. It is hardly a mere coincidence that several members of the Workers' Opposition—the first, the most uncompromising and the most single-minded in their rejection of bureaucratism—were later to become officials in Stalin's administration and even escaped the purges. Their principles were so high that there was

---

[16] *New Left Review*, 44, p. 83. It is clear that in the thirties, the manner in which collectivization was conducted as a campaign made many of Stalin's functionaries dubious of their leader. It was then that Stalin eliminated those whose creation he had been, and substituted them with those who were his creations. In this way, he may be said to have carried out part of Trotsky's program. Young people, most of them of working-class origin, took the places of the Old Guard. (They later became leaders of the country—Nikita Khrushchev, Georgy Malenkov, and others). The overwhelming majority of the 1934 Congress, the Congress of Victors, were purged. This was sociologically the main change, in fact, camouflaged by the spectacular show trials of the former Left and Right Opposition; the trial of those who had become politically insignificant. The party and state functionaries never gained the opportunity to become a stable, permanent social group under Stalin.

[17] It was in this same 1918 article that Lenin wrote against those who believed that it was a mistake to have taken power:

> Such an argument could be advanced only by the "man in the muffler" who forgets that there will never be "conformity," that it cannot exist either in the development of society or in the development of nature, that only by a series of attempts, each of which taken by itself will be one-sided—will suffer from certain inconsistencies—will victorious socialism be created by the revolutionary cooperation of the proletariat of *all* countries.

no possibility of living up to them (a human situation in which Feodor Dostoyevsky had been very interested). Hence, later, nothing came to matter to them. Lenin's opposition to bureaucratic and administrative étatism, represented at first mainly by Trotsky, was realistic. But these representatives of the Workers' Opposition, once they had perceived that their aims were unreal, found it easier to accept Stalin's version of realism than many others.

This is very relevant to what Mandel calls Lenin's "main final battle and preoccupation during the last period of his life" —the struggle against bureaucracy. For Lenin never precisely posed the problem idealistically, with the either/or of political romanticism. It was not for Lenin a question of bureaucracy or no bureaucracy. Lenin was acutely aware of the insurmountable contradictions that dominated both internal and external policy. He believed that the only way to deal with them was by a policy of deliberate experimentation. The bureaucratic and authoritarian tendencies had to be fought, but compromises were inevitable in the course of this struggle. Lenin's aim was not the impossible one of complete triumph over bureaucratism; it was rather that he was looking for *correctives* to it. This is the significance of his crucial role in the trade union debates, when he resolutely opposed Bukharin's and Trotsky's étatistic policies, and insisted that the trade unions had to be in a position to defend the workers against the actual Soviet state:

> Comrade Trotsky speaks of the workers' state. Permit me, this is an abstraction. . . . Our present state is such that the inclusively organized proletariat must defend itself and must utilize these workers' organizations for the defense of the workers against the state and for the defense of our state by the workers.

Lenin never idealized this state. In 1921, he wrote: "The workers' state is an abstraction. In reality we have a workers' state with the following peculiar features: (1) it is the peasants and not the workers who predominate in the population; (2) it is a workers' state with bureaucratic deformations." It is noticeable that Lenin found it necessary to qualify the notion "workers' state" even beyond indicating its bureaucratic deformations. He was intensely conscious of the need to grasp the *specificity* of the Russian situation. "Bureaucratism" *tout court* was as abstract as

the notion of a "workers' state." But vulgar Marxism dominated the thinking of the leading cadres of the party. No new
historical situation can ever be properly grasped by means of
vulgar Marxism; but there were hardly any circumstances for
which it was so inadequate as those of Russia in the twenties.
From the vulgar Marxist standpoint, there was no solution: the
party should have given up. Bukharin and many others sought
refuge in zigzags between extreme right and extreme left positions;
the background was a kind of despair. Bukharin wept in 1918,
when the party decided to accept food from the Americans, and
said to Trotsky; "They are turning the party into a dung
heap." [18] Trotsky and Stalin reacted differently to this situation,
according to the character of their respective Marxisms. They
had an advantage compared with the other leaders in their overwhelming voluntarism. But this took opposing forms. What is
relevant here is merely to note that Trotsky's Marxism cannot be
defined as the positive obverse of Stalin's. Mechanical pairing of
the two does not necessarily advance our understanding of either.
There was a nemesis in Stalin's Marxism; but it does not modify
or subtract from the nemesis in Trotsky's. "Sociologism" and
"power politics" are both fundamental departures from Leninism.

3. Russia and World Revolution

The debate—"socialism in one country versus permanent
revolution"—forms the focus of Mandel's final comments on my
essay. They provide an occasion to clarify some recurring misconceptions about the history of the international revolutionary

---

[18] Anatoly Lunacharsky once commented on Trotsky's personality:
"Trotsky treasures his revolutionary role and would probably be ready to
make any personal sacrifice, not excluding the greatest sacrifice of all, that
of his life, in order to go down in human memory surrounded by the
aureole of a genuine revolutionary leader." There is something in this.
Trotsky was given to "dramatic" politics and statements that were not
always justifiable by any sober criteria. It might be said that his tragedy
was of a Schillerian type, as opposed to the tragedy of Lenin's last years.
It will be remembered that Marx and Engels criticized Ferdinand Lassalle's
Sickingen drama, categorizing it as Schillerian in comparison with Shake-
spearean drama.

movement since the twenties. Mandel argues that Trotsky had coherent domestic and international policies, both founded on the fundamental theses of "permanent revolution." He does not explicitly challenge my analysis of the conflations on which the notion of permanent revolution was built. Given this, it may be assumed that the analysis stands. What he does contest is that Trotsky's polemics against socialism in one country implied any belief that the Soviet Union would collapse because of the "subversion" of the world market or military aggression. He also argues that Trotsky's economic policy of accelerated industrialization was accompanied by a political policy for the different social classes in the U.S.S.R.—a correct "handling of contradictions among the people." But on both of these points, the evidence is overwhelming. In his brochure *Permanent Revolution* (1928), Trotsky says: "The crises of the Soviet economy are not merely maladies of growth, a sort of infantile sickness, but something far more significant—they are the harsh curbings of the world market." [19] His whole discussion here assumes that the capitalist world market is the economic system rendering socialism impossible in one country—yet he never concretely explains why or how. The same is true of his discussion of military intervention from abroad. He writes:

> Either the proletariat comes to power or else the bourgeoisie, by a series of crushing blows, weakens the revolutionary pressure to regain freedom of action, above all in the question of war and peace. Only a reformist can picture the pressure of the proletariat upon the bourgeois state as a permanently increasing factor and as a guarantee against intervention. [20]

It is clear from the context of his pamphlet that he was thinking of an economic or military collapse of the U.S.S.R., as the curiously Khrushchevite proviso he added shows: "The example of a backward country, which in the course of several five-year plans was able to construct a mighty socialist society with its own forces, would mean a deathblow to world capitalism and would reduce to a minimum, if not to zero, the costs of world proletarian

---

[19] *Permanent Revolution*, p. 30.
[20] *Ibid.*, p. 143.

revolution." Stalin, of course, never claimed anything like this.[21] Once again, the assumption that the isolated Soviet state was not in the long run viable is the only one that makes the statement meaningful.

Given this, it is quite logical that Trotsky's political policy for domestic industrialization should have been so vague: it was a sort of emergency measure until the advent of international revolution saved the situation. Mandel himself provides the proof of this when he quotes the Left Opposition's alternative to the massive upheaval of Stalin's industrialization: "a special tax on rich peasants only, and a radical reduction of administrative expenses, economizing one billion gold rubles annually." [22] The academic, if not demagogic, character of such a proposal is patent. Financing accumulation by reducing state expenditure is a utopian dream in any backward country. It is difficult to believe Trotsky himself took the proposal seriously. Certainly, it had no relation whatever to the desperate economic situation of 1928, which was one of virtual blockade of the towns by the kulaks, as E. H. Carr has recently pointed out ("Revolution from Above," *New Left Review*, 46). Trotsky's program for industrialization, for all its economic prescience, contains no political solution for the problem of the peasantry. Hence it was always open to confiscation by Stalin, and insertion into a war against the kulaks. The prompt realignment of Evgeny Preobrazhensky and Grigory Piatakov in 1929 is the evidence of this; had there been an agreed *political* formula for the opposition's industrialization program, such a switch could not have occurred.

The international perspective of "permanent revolution" was the ultimate rationale for this incomplete internal policy. Mandel's interpretation of this concept must now be considered. He rejects the idea that it can essentially be identified with belief in the

---

[21] *Ibid.*, p. 26. I said in my first essay that Stalin's perspective in this issue was superior to Trotsky's. Russia's isolation was a fact. But that was not the end of the matter. During the Central Committee discussion of the Peace Treaty with Germany in January, 1918, Stalin said that where Western revolutionary movements were concerned, there were no facts, only possibilities, and possibilities could not be taken into account. "Not be taken into account?" Lenin asked. This was a decisive difference between the two, then and later. Lenin never ignored facts, but he always took possibilities into account.

[22] *New Left Review*, 47, p. 44.

imminence and ubiquity of insurrection. On the contrary, he argues, all it implies is that the historical *epoch* is one of frequent reproduction of revolutionary situations, none of which need necessarily produce a successful seizure of power. The geographical limits of the concept remain undefined, but presumably they extend to the whole globe. Now if this interpretation is to be given to the concept of "permanent revolution," it ceases to be wrong, and merely becomes banal. For who in the Comintern would ever have denied that the historical epoch was characterized by the periodic upsurge of revolutionary situations? No statement could be safer or less controversial. An "epoch" comprises a great many years—it is numbered in decades. Eruptions may be spaced very widely within such a time span, and still be "periodic." The dilution of permanent revolution leads to its banalization.

Mandel's account of the concept, however, includes one polemical corollary. He argues that because there were numerous revolutionary situations in Europe after 1919 and none produced a socialist revolution, therefore the responsibility for these failures should essentially be attributed to the Comintern and to the Soviet party that controlled it. "The main responsibility for the working-class defeats of the twenties, thirties, and early forties can be put squarely at the door of inadequate leadership." [23] Permanent revolution here becomes the rationale for a historical indictment of Soviet foreign policy. There is no doubt that this is an accurate interpretation of Trotsky's vision of the thirties. But is it an accurate account of history? Mandel rightly criticizes psychological explanations of Stalin's policies, and calls for sociological explanations. But he does not see that he merely repeats the error on a different level when he tries to attribute every important revolutionary defeat since 1922 to the policies of the U.S.S.R. This was precisely Trotsky's mistake, and it derived from his constant underestimation of the importance of the nation as a political institution.[24] The fact is that the Comintern did not in the last instance determine the fate of the revolutionary movements of every country of the world. This should be obvious to any Marxist. To believe otherwise is to exaggerate out of all

----

[23] *New Left Review*, 47, p. 48.
[24] There is an instructive contrast between Trotsky and Lenin here. A good example may be seen in their attitudes toward Norway and Serbia,

proportion the importance and influence of the nascent Soviet state on world affairs. The vulgar anticommunist conviction that the "Kremlin" was responsible for every eruption of social discontent or revolution anywhere in the world here finds its vulgar Marxist opposite: the Kremlin becomes responsible for every suppression of social discontent and every victory of counter-revolution. This is a notion incompatible with any rational appreciation of world history. It is founded precisely on the sociological monism for which I criticized Trotsky: the assumption of a "planetary social structure, soaring above its articulation in any concrete political system." The voluntarist consequence is the attribution of a malefic omnipotence to the U.S.S.R. Thus Mandel does not hesitate to write that the "fifty million victims of the Second World War" were the "result" of Comintern policy. The idealism of this trend of thought, and its distance from Marxism, are evident.

Once counterrevolutionary dominance is internationally attributed to Stalin, there is no longer any objective restraint on the location of "revolutionary situations" whose triumph the Soviet Union is alleged to have prevented. Near-misses multiply in

---

respectively, in the two World Wars. Trotsky wrote of Norway in 1940, when the Germans had invaded it:

> Two governments struggle for a while in Norway: the government of the Norwegian Nazis, covered by the German troops in the South, and the old Social-Democratic government with their king in the North. What is involved in Norway is the direct and immediate clash between two imperialist camps, in whose hands the warring Norwegian governments are only auxiliary tools. On the world arena we support neither the camp of the allies nor the camp of Germany. Consequently we have not the slightest reason or justification for supporting either one of their temporary tools within Norway itself. *In Defense of Marxism*, pp. 171–172.

In other words, he refused to perceive the relative justice of the Norwegian national cause against the Germans. He was mechanically and abstractly reproducing the classical revolutionary positions on World War I, despite the evident differences between them. Lenin, in 1914, by contrast, based his whole politics on an absolute condemnation of the World War as an interimperialist struggle; but he said that there was a relative justice in the Serbian national struggle against the Austro-Hungarian and German Empires. He spoke of their predatory expedition against Serbia. His Marxism was always dialectical; it integrated both the principal and the secondary contradictions.

Mandel's text: no less than four for Germany, three for Spain, three for France and even, perhaps, one for Britain—all of them "revolutionary situations." The merest glance at the list shows how remote from history it is. The British general strike was hailed by Trotsky at the time as the signal for a general revolutionary uprising. Yet the organized British working class failed to demonstrate any "instinctive drive to take society's fate into their own hands." It fought for strictly limited objectives, and resigned itself to an absolute defeat of them. (The British Communist Party showed an accurate appreciation of the conjuncture, which contrasts with Trotsky's mistake.) The 1945 situation in France and Italy made an armed bid for power by the national communist parties very problematic. The fate of Greece is the evidence. There, the Left was very much stronger than in France or Italy; and the country was much less vital to imperialism than France or Italy. The Greek revolution was nevertheless ruthlessly crushed by Anglo-American invasion. Maurice Thorez and Palmiro Togliatti had much less chance than the KKE. The Spanish Civil War is another example. Mandel implies that the Spanish Communists could have made a successful revolution within the embattled Republic in 1936–37 and then gone on to military victory over Franco. Yet they were only a small minority of the Republican forces at the time, which themselves had little chance of winning the war once the military relationship of forces crystallized in 1936. The possibilities of a socialist revolution in Germany were also remote. The KPD at no time had anything like the force to deal with the Wehrmacht—rearmed and equipped by the social democrats for the deliberate purpose of counterrevolution in 1918, and constantly enlarged thereafter. This strategic situation was prior to any consideration of Nazism. A successful check to Nazism was one thing; a proletarian revolution, quite another.

Of course, Stalin's policies were wrong in France, Italy, and, above all, Germany. I emphasized in my original essay the successive blunders of the Third International. Moreover, Trotsky's critique of the Comintern policies in Germany was excellent (it is perhaps significant, incidentally, that his best polemics of these years were written from a rightist position, paralled to that of Brandler, not from a leftist position, which he adopted during the Popular Fronts). But in all these cases, Stalin's international policies were ultimately a secondary factor within a contest fought and decided at the *national* level. The primary unit of class struggle was the nation; the promulgation of Comintern policies in Moscow did nothing to alter this. Stalin's international policies became decisive only when the nation as such was abolished—in war. Then, precisely, with the cancellation of national frontiers and the temporary dissolution of the social structures that they enclosed, the role of Soviet actions became supreme. The Red Army in Eastern Europe, when it created a *cordon sanitaire* in reverse, achieved what no Comintern directive ever had any possibility of doing.

The fundamental mistake Trotsky made in underestimating the autonomy of the political institution of the nation state is evident in his whole assumption that, because of "incorrect Comintern policies," no revolution was possible within the ranks of the parties loyal to the Third International. Yet it was precisely this belief that was spectacularly disproved, thereby confirming— *a contrario*—how secondary the impact of these policies was on the revolutionary contest within any given country. The monumental upheaval of the Chinese Revolution—not to speak of other victories in Vietnam, Yugoslavia, and Albania—showed this definitively. The Chinese Revolution, the fundamental turning point in world history of these decades, focuses all the main errors that haunted Trotsky's thinking. It was a victorious revolution led by a party that never openly challenged or defied the Comintern or Stalin. This was something Trotsky believed impossible—hence his decision to create a new International. It was based on the country and its main-force strength was the peasantry, yet it never abandoned its socialist program or ideology. Trotsky explicitly condemned Mao and the Chinese party for retreating to rural China after 1927, and predicted that they would degenerate into a mere peasant movement. No more obvious instance of Trotsky's sociologism may be conceived.[25] This was his judgment of the

---

[25] Trotsky's dismissal of the Chinese Revolution contrasts very revealingly with the importance he gave trivial American intellectuals and the small political groups they represented. The sociologism that led him to discount the Chinese Party as a peasant phenomenon induced him to believe that the American working class—because it was the proletariat of the most advanced capitalist country—was a decisive historical force in the thirties, and therefore ideological disputes on its margin were of tremendous significance. Hence the indignity of his debates with Burnham, Schachtman, and others (heightened by his private awareness of their nullity).

decisive political phenomenon of the epoch, and it reveals with the utmost clarity his constant tendency to translate political institutions immediately into social forces—and the momentous mistakes such a theoretical deviation produces. (It may be added that Trotsky's writings on China show his incomprehension of the revolutionary potential of guerrilla warfare, which he had learned to subordinate as Commander of the Red Army: here Lenin and Mao were both, at different moments of time, his superior.) Trotsky thus never became properly aware of the tremendous victories of the Long March and the Anti-Japanese War. The categories of his Marxism prevented him from understanding these all-important events. His earlier lucidity on China was of no avail once Mao won the leadership of the Chinese party and reoriented its whole historical course. Henceforth the Chinese experience, which was to be the vortex of world revolution at mid-century, escaped him.

It escaped Stalin too, of course. But this is precisely the point. Stalin's policies were not Furies, with the power of life and death over the world revolutionary movement. They were the cautious and conservative moves of the Soviet state, which necessarily had only a limited influence over events elsewhere—except when the state overran its national boundaries, in 1944–45. Stalin's policies were not ultimately responsible for the failure of revolution in the West—any more than they were for the success of revolution in the East. Those parties with enough vitality to ignore Comintern advice were those which had enough combative power to win the revolution; those which docilely complied with mistaken directives of the Comintern were not those likely to rout the bourgeoisie. The fact that Stalin was so often wrong in these years does not thereby mean that Trotsky was conversely right. Leninism had disappeared with its author, and the charges and counter-charges of these decades echoed and reechoed in the gulf of its absence.

Summary

To sum up: Trotsky's indifference to political institutions divided him from Lenin before the October Revolution, and excluded him from the Bolshevik party. His previous theory and practice then isolated him within the party in the twenties, and ultimately ensured his defeat. In the thirties, his abstract inter-nationalism prevented him from understanding the complex in-tranational dynamics that governed the main development of the different detachments of the world revolutionary movement. Trot-sky's sociologism forms a consistent unity. It should not be nec-essary to say that a critique of his theoretical and political practice does not in any way detract from his extraordinary achievements during the October Revolution and the Civil War. On the con-trary, as my essay stressed, the two were organically united: Trotsky had all the virtues of his vices.

This is true of the last period of his life. I wrote that these years were "dominated by his symbolic relationship to the great drama of the previous decade, which had become for him a tragic fate. His activities became most futile." But this was not the futility of theatrical gestures and tactical accommodations of the twenties. It was no longer an absence of perspective. In his new impasse, he found a certain greatness. The split between the "ought" and the "is" had an objective historical basis in the thirties. Trotsky's "ought" was nevertheless valid, in that the marriage of socialism with nationalism and an autocratic system is an absurdity. But by then there was no possibility of its achiev-ing determinate historical existence. Trotsky became a myth by identifying himself with this "ought." It was Engels who wrote that although the utopian socialists were wrong in an economic sense, they represented a truth in an ultimate, world-historical sense. Something similar may be said of Trotsky. Mandel claims that he represented the "Principles of Soviet democracy and revolutionary internationalism." Reality, however, is never merely a matter of principles. The price Trotsky had to pay for his stature was to become unreal—a romantic myth and symbol. He was a revolu-tionary on a classical scale. His survival into a postclassical age and arena was his tragedy. It is well to restate this fundamental category. For Marxism is not a beatific optimism: it is the intel-ligence of an intolerable era and the movement to transform it.

ERNEST MANDEL

"Trotsky's Marxism": A Rejoinder

Nicolas Krassó attempted to explain Stalin's victory in the inner-party struggle of the Bolshevik party during the twenties by two alleged basic weaknesses of "Trotsky's Marxism": his "sociologism," i.e., his constant underestimation of the autonomous role of political institutions; and his "administrativism," which tended to identify him with the stringent repressive measures the Bolshevik regime had to introduce against the working class in the 1920–21 period. We showed that these explanations do not correspond to historical truth and do not give an adequate explanation of the destiny of the Russian Revolution after 1917—not to speak of the destiny of world revolution.

In his reply, Krassó tries to defend his hypothesis both by general theoretical arguments and by an attempt to refute some of the factual material I introduced into the discussion.[1] Both attempts fail. They illustrate more clearly than Krassó's initial piece the basic weakness of his analysis, which consists in departing from the Marxist method of understanding, interpreting, and acting upon contemporary history.

---

[1] *New Left Review*, 44, 47, 48.

Empiricism and Marxist Historiography: A first approach

"The whole aim of my analysis was to try and reconstruct the unity of Trotsky's thought and practice as a Marxist: its singular character and coherence. Mandel's reply renounces any attempt to seek such a unity," writes Krassó.[2] In other words, Krassó tries to view Trotsky's thought and practice as a totality governed by some basic principles, which he seeks to discover. Any refusal to answer him on the same level—either to accept his definition of the *uniqueness* of Trotsky's Marxism, or to substitute another "basic principle" for his own to interpret Trotsky—is condemned as "empiricism."

We shall come back at the end of this essay to what we consider the *differentia specifica* of Trotsky's Marxism. But let us first take Krassó's theoretical argument for what it is worth. From the point of view of Marxian dialectics, processes are governed not by basic ideas but by *conflicting forces*. Any historical process is governed by basic contradictions of a social nature. To conceive of a life process essentially ruled and explained by ideas is to take a step backward from Marx to Hegel. To view these ideas as immutable, permanent, and unrelated either to their inner contradictions or to the contradictions between them and living practice is to take a step backward from Hegel to Kant.

To assume that Trotsky's life constitutes a "unity" whose key is an ideological "conception"; to identify that conception with the original sin of "sociologism"; to deny the historical fact that, after joining the Bolshevik party, Trotsky attached the greatest importance to the role of the "subjective factor" in history and politics, became the staunchest defender of the Leninist theory of the party, and gave us, both as a politician and a historian, some of the finest examples of precise understanding of the "autonomous role of political institutions," is to advance an "explanation" for Trotsky's Marxism that flies in the face of truth. It is an arbitrary, abstract construction of the mind, divorced from reality, both theoretical and practical.

The methodological weakness of Krassó's thesis goes deeper

---

[2] *New Left Review*, 48, p. 90.

than his failure to explain in a consistent way all the essential aspects of Trotsky's activities (the superiority of dialectical theory over empiricism does not reside in its negation of empirical data, but in its capacity to explain them in a coherent manner; and no coherent explanation of Trotsky's theory and action in, say, 1917, 1923, 1933, or 1938 is possible from the viewpoint of his "underestimating the autonomous role of political institutions"). This weakness goes to the roots of one of the most fascinating aspects of Marxist sociology and historiography: the relationship between the individual and the historical process.

We do not deny that every individual can be considered as a relevant object of study, that his life process can be dialectically examined and explained. But obviously, what we are practicing in such theoretical activity is individual psychology, not sociology.[3] This procedure is all right as long as we are dealing with individuals who play only a marginal role in the historical process. The great contribution of Marx toward understanding history was precisely the point that one cannot explain the historical process as a simple interaction of individual psychologies, as a myriad of intertwining "case histories." What this understanding demands is a conceptual *social* mediation: that of the social class. World history is not a history of conflicting individuals (although these individuals are very real and sometimes very important); world history is a history of *class struggle*. The combination of individual aspirations, needs, strivings, and ideas, which are relevant for the understanding of history, is their combination in social classes. The conflicts that shape history in civilized life are the conflicts between social classes or within social classes.[4]

---

[3] We don't hereby imply that social factors should be eliminated from those that shape an individual's life process. But they act within a different framework, on a different level, and in relation to a different totality when used to explain an individual career than when they are conceived as forces that shape the destinies of nations or of mankind.

[4] The rationale of this distinction has been convincingly stated by Engels in his letter to Joseph Block of September 21–22, 1890:

> History is made in such a way that the final result always arises from conflicts between many individuals wills, of which each in turn has been made what it is by a host of particular conditions of life. Thus there are innumerable intersecting forces, an infinite series of parallelograms of forces which give rise to one resultant—the his-

Individuals who play a key role in history can do so only because they succeed in expressing, in a superior way, at a decisive turning point, the needs and aspirations of social formations. Once the unique relationship of social forces that propels them onto the historical scene is fundamentally modified, their historical role is finished.[5]

Any assessment of Trotsky starts out on the wrong foot if it tries to discover in Trotsky's "inner thought"—i.e., in one aspect of the *individual*—the explanation of his role in *history*. We do not deny the usefulness of completing historical analysis by individual psychology, although up to now what we possess on that score is rather unconvincing. We deny most strongly the possibility of

---

torical event. This may again itself be viewed as the product of a power which works as a whole unconsciously and without volition. For what each individual wills is obstructed by everyone else, and what emerges is something that no one willed. Thus history has proceeded hitherto in the manner of a natural process and is essentially subject to the same laws of motion. But from the fact that the wills of individuals . . . do not attain what they want, but are merged into an aggregate mean, a common resultant, it must not be concluded that they are equal to zero. On the contrary, each contributes to the resultant and is to this extent included in it. (Marx-Engels, *Selected Correspondence* [Moscow: Progress Publishers, 1965], p. 418)

See also Lenin:

By examining the *totality* of opposing tendencies, by reducing them to precisely definable conditions of life and production of the various *classes* of society, by discarding subjectivism and arbitrariness in the choice of a particular "dominant" idea or its interpretation, and by revealing that, without exception, all ideas and all the various tendencies *stem* from the condition of the material forces of production, Marxism indicated the way to an all-embracing and comprehensive study of the process of the rise, development and decline of socio-economic systems. People make their own history, but what determines the motives of people, of the mass of the people, i.e. what gives rise to the clash of conflicting ideas and strivings? (*Collected Works,* Vol. 21 [Moscow: Progress Publishers, 1964], p. 57)

[5] Cf. "That such and such a man and precisely that man arises at a particular time in a particular country is, of course, pure chance. But cut him out and there will be a demand for a substitute, and this substitute will be found, good or bad, but in the long run he will be found." (Engels' letter to H. Starkenburg of January 25, 1894, in Marx-Engels, *Selected Correspondence,* p. 467)

explaining history through individual psychology. The political struggle in the Soviet Union in the twenties, the political struggle in the world communist movement in the twenties and the thirties, involved the destinies of hundreds of millions of human beings. To explain the outcome of a conflict of such dimensions by the personal idiosyncrasies of this or that individual—X had a persecution mania; Y had a stomach ulcer; Z "underestimated the autonomous role of political institutions"—is not only un-Marxist it is ludicrous.

Here is Krassó's basic weakness. On this point his "Reply to Ernest Mandel" does not offer any additional material. We hear a lot about what Trotsky and Lenin did or did not think and do at this or that stage of the political and social struggle in the Soviet Union. However, we are given no explanation at all of the ups and downs of revolution *in relation to social forces,* either in Russia or on the world scale. And when Krassó makes a timid attempt to introduce such an explanation of an episodic aspect of the whole problem—the trade union dispute of 1921—he goes to the length of denying the very physical existence of social classes, in this case the proletariat. Under such circumstances, there is no room for scientific historiography. Krassó's failure to understand "Trotsky's Marxism" ends in an abandonment of Marxism itself.

Lenin, Trotsky, and the Theory of the Party

Krassó is astonished by our statement that "it was Lenin, not Trotsky, who to a large extent borrowed from the theoreticians of German and Austrian social democracy in his theory of party organization." Astonishment is of course no proof. Neither is the attempt to identify Lenin's theory of the party with the concept of professional revolutionaries nor the assertion that "there is no evidence that at any state thereafter—(after first not understanding it—E. M.)—Trotsky genuinely learned the lesson of Lenin's theory of the party." [6]

Krassó does not seem to remember that the concept of professional revolutionaries is not the basic premise of Lenin's theory

---

[6] *New Left Review,* 48, p. 91.

of the party; this is only a consequence that flows from other basic assumptions. He himself earlier correctly defined Lenin's "fundamental thesis" in his theory of the revolutionary party as meaning that socialism as a theory had to be brought to the working class from the outside through a party that included the revolutionary intelligentsia.[7] It is that "fundamental thesis" that we said had been inspired by Viktor Adler and Karl Kautsky. And if Krassó would make the effort to read the sources we quoted, he would have to admit that the essential elements of Lenin's theory of the revolutionary party had indeed been produced by German (and Austro-German) social democracy in the early nineties.

Lenin himself never made a secret of his conviction that his theory of the party was inspired by German social democracy. There are, of course, exaggerations in these allegations by Lenin of his close ideological affiliation with Kautsky and Co.; they were made in the heat of a faction fight. It is also true that Lenin, when he returned to the same subject after the experience of the 1905 Revolution, used formulations that were more integrated than those used in *What Is to Be Done?* (in *Selected Works* [New York: International Publishers, 1943]), especially in regard to the necessary integration between the vanguard party and the class; we indicated these in our first reply to Krassó.

But all this is beside the point. What we stressed was the fact that Lenin's organizational concept, before 1917, was closer than Trotsky's to that of social democracy. The origin of this closeness is very clear: Lenin, as well as the Social Democrats, stressed the leading role the *organized* workers had to play with regard to the *unorganized* ones; Trotsky underestimated the importance of that organization. But, together with Rosa Luxemburg, he understood earlier than Lenin that organization is in itself no guarantee for *revolutionary* leadership; that it can even become a trap that prevents the working class from going forward on the road of revolution. He had a keen presentiment of the *potential conservatism* of a party apparatus. Any Marxist theory of the party that brushes this aside as "sociologism" does not understand anything about the history of the working-class movement since 1914.

---

[7] *New Left Review*, 44, p. 66.

We say purposely: since 1914. What is completely missing from Krassó's analysis is an estimate of Lenin's attitude toward the party and the International as defined by the traumatic experience Lenin underwent after August 4, 1914. This "hiatus" in Krassó's analysis is not accidental. By passing over Lenin's writings on social democracy, he conveniently eliminates what became the cornerstone of Leninism from that date on: *the combination of a theory of the party with a revolutionary program and practice.* Without such a combination, party "organization" not only becomes an empty shell, from the viewpoint of the class struggle; it may become a potential vehicle of hostile social forces. When Krassó actually reproaches Trotsky for "fetishization of the program in Trotsky's later thought," and counterposes to that "the structure of the party that was the anchor of Lenin's thought," [8] he objectively slanders Trotsky as well as Lenin. After joining the Bolsheviks, Trotsky never divorced the program from the structure of the party. After 1914, Lenin never divorced the structure of the party from the revolutionary program and practice; he had learned his lesson on August 4, 1914. [9]

It would lead us too far afield to enumerate here all the instances where Trotsky, after March, 1917, expressed his understanding of Lenin's theory of the party, not only in theory but in practice. [10] We shall limit ourselves to one quotation:

---

[8] *New Left Review*, 48, p. 92.

[9] Cf. Lenin:

In Europe, socialism has emerged from a comparatively peaceful stage that is confined within narrow and national limits. With the outbreak of the war of 1914–15 it entered the stage of revolutionary action; there can be no doubt that the time has come for a complete break with opportunism, for its expulsion from the workers' parties . . . The building of a revolutionary organization must be begun— that is demanded by the new historical situation, by the epoch of proletarian revolutionary action—but it can be begun only *over the heads* of the old leaders, the stranglers of revolutionary energy, *over the heads* of the old party, through its *destruction.* (*Collected Works*, Vol. 21, pp. 249, 252–253).

[10] Cf. his attitude toward Levi's split with the KPD in 1921; his attitude toward the key role of the party in the revolutionary crisis of summer-autumn 1923 in Germany; his attitude toward the absolute necessity of preserving the autonomy of the Chinese CP in 1926–27, etc., etc.

The initiating minority, to whom the syndicalist theory assigns the leadership, actually placing it above the mass trade union organizations of the proletariat, cannot remain formless. But if this initiating minority of the working class is correctly organized; if it is bound by internal discipline, corresponding to the implacable demands of the revolutionary epoch; if it is armed with the correct doctrine, the scientifically constructed doctrine of the proletarian revolution—then we shall obtain nothing other than the Communist Party, standing above the syndicates as well as above all other forms of the labor movement, fructifying them ideologically and directing all their work.

. . . Hence flows the iron necessity of creating the French Communist Party which must wholly absorb both the existing revolutionary wing of the Socialist Party as well as the revolutionary detachment of French syndicalism. The party must create its own apparatus, absolutely independent, rigidly centralized, and separate and apart from both the present Socialist Party as well as the CGT and the local syndicates.

. . . The way out is: to undertake immediately the building of the centralized Communist Party and, above all, to establish immediately in the chief centers of the labor movement daily newspapers which—in contrast to the existing dailies—will not be organs of internal organizational criticism and abstract propaganda, but organs of direct revolutionary agitation for, and political leadership of, the struggle of the proletarian masses.[11]

It would be hard for anyone, including Nicolas Krassó, to conjure up any difference between Lenin's theory of the party expressed in *What Is to Be Done?* and this statement of Trotsky's made in 1920.

The Content of the 1923 Options

In his attempt to present Trotsky as a "romantic myth and symbol," the greatest stumbling block for Krassó is the concrete and precise alternative course that Trotsky proposed both to the Russian Bolshevik party and to the Communist International

---

[11] *On the Coming Congress of the Comintern,* July 22, 1920, in Leon Trotsky, *The First Years of the Communist International,* Vol. I (New York: Pioneer Publishers, 1945), pp. 93–94.

during the 1923–33 period. Krassó began by constructing a baseless "contradiction" between the theory of permanent revolution, as interpreted by Krassó, and Trotsky's fight for accelerated industrialization inside the Soviet Union. We showed that where Krassó only saw inconsistency—which precisely proved the inconsistency of his attempts at "interpreting" Trotsky—there was a logical interrelationship: a conscious drive to strengthen the weight of the proletariat, both nationally and internationally.

In his "Reply to Ernest Mandel," Krassó goes a step further and simply denies that Trotsky and the Left Opposition presented any kind of an alternative program to Stalin's policies in the twenties. In order to bolster this preposterous proposition, he resorts to some transparent sleight-of-hand in the matter of chronology: because the Soviet proletariat's numbers were reduced by two-thirds in *1921,* the policy of gradual mobilization and repolitization of that proletariat in *1923–24* was unrealistic, and Trotsky's proposals for accelerated industrial accumulation "had no relation whatsoever to the desperate economic situation of *1928,* which was one of virtual blockade of the towns by the kulaks." [12] One is rather dumbfounded by this kind of "logic."

Let us admit that the proletariat was really reduced by two-thirds in 1921 (we have more than doubts on the reliability of these figures; we shall try to prove some other time that they are grossly exaggerated). But surely, in 1923, not to speak of 1926, the proletariat did not remain "disintegrated and dispersed," to repeat Krassó's terms.[13] According to official Soviet statistics, quoted by Solomon Schwartz, the number of wage and salary earners, which had risen from 7.9 million to 11.2 million between 1897 and 1913, fell to 6.6 million in 1922/23 and then rose rapidly to 7.4 million in 1923/24, 10.2 million in 1924/25, 10.9 million in 1925/27, and 11.6 million in 1928. In large-scale industry the number of workers, which had fallen from 2.8 million in 1913 to 1.7 million in 1922/23, rose to 1.8 million in 1923/24, 2.2 million in 1924/25, 2.7 million in 1925/26, 2.8 million in 1926/27, and 3.1 million in 1928. The number of building workers rose steeply from 200,000 in 1923/24 to 550,000 in 1926/27 and 700,000 in 1928. Given the fact that the prewar figures include a

12 *New Left Review,* 48, p. 99.
13 *Ibid.,* p. 95.

very large number of domestic personnel (over 2 million) and that this category had dwindled to around 200,000 in the twenties, one can say that around 1926 the industrial proletariat in the proper sense of the word had already passed beyond the prerevolutionary level. This is indeed a far cry from a "disintegrated and dispersed" proletariat![14]

Still, granting that the proletariat was actually "reduced by two-thirds" in 1921, what the above-quoted figures show is obviously a *process* of numerical, economic, and social *reconstitution* of the proletariat from 1921 to 1928. Surely nobody can deny that a social class that produces over sixty percent of the national income (that was the situation as early as 1926) has potential social power. But Trotsky, we must remind Krassó, did not propose immediately to restore the role of the working class in leading the state and the economy in 1921, when it was economically and socially reduced to its weakest state. That was the politically wrong and unrealistic position of the "Workers' Opposition," which Trotsky rejected out of hand. An upturn in and a physical revival of the working class were necessary preconditions for its revival as a politically ruling class. For these reasons, Trotsky firmly and correctly supported the turn toward the New Economic Policy and the immediate priorities given to economic revival.

But this was only the beginning of a process. Once the economy started to function again, real wages rose, the number of wage earners increased, and their weight in the economy again became decisive because of the steep increase in industrial production, then the objective conditions for a revival of the *political* role of the proletariat once again appeared. At that point, the conscious intervention of the party could either favor such a revival or act as powerful brake. The program of the Left Opposition was a consistent attempt to facilitate such a revival by proposing to suppress unemployment, accelerate industrialization, increase the scope of Soviet Democracy, favor self-expression and self-activity of the toiling masses, and strengthen the chances of international revolution which, in turn, would raise the self-confidence and militancy of the Soviet workers.

---

[14] Solomon Schwartz, *Les Ouvriers en Union Sovietique* (Paris: Rivière, 1956), pp. 50–53.

By maintaining mass unemployment and mass manipulation of the "soviets" more and more divorced from any substantial role in administering the state and the economy, by whittling away the remnants of workers' democracy outside the party and the strong traditions of inner-party democracy as well, the ruling faction did everything possible to lower the militancy and self-activity of the proletariat. That is the objective balance sheet of the confrontation.

When Krassó writes: "This was the nub of the problem: not the 'passivity' of the proletariat (Mandel's phrase)—a subjective conjunctural state, but its disintegration and dispersal—an objective structural condition," [15] he makes an excellent summary of the problem and, at the same time, provides an implicit answer that destroys his own thesis. It is obviously impossible to argue that "disintegration and dispersal" were an "objective, structural condition" between 1923 and 1928, when industrial output was rising toward and beyond the prerevolutionary level. The *objective possibility* of overcoming the "subjective conjunctural state" of passivity after 1923 did exist. If it was not achieved, that was due to the key role of the party. Any other interpretation, in the face of the given facts, seriously "underestimates the autonomous role of political institutions"; this we can now squarely and rightly lay at Krassó's feet.

On the Left Opposition's program of financing investment through a special tax on rich peasants and Nepmen only, and a reduction of state expenditure, Krassó has this comment to make: "Financing accumulation by reducing state expenditure is a utopian dream in any backward country!" [16] One might as well say that socialist revolution and building up a Soviet state in a backward country is a "utopian dream," too; many Mensheviks, old and young, would of course agree with Krassó there. One wonders whether Krassó has ever read Lenin's *State and Revolution* (in *Collected Works* [New York: n.d.]) and its extensive remarks on the "cheap state"; whether he ever read Lenin's *The Economic Catastrophe and the Way to Fight Against It,* as well as numerous other writings. Probably the Lenin who wrote all

---

[15] *New Left Review,* 48, p. 95.
[16] *New Left Review,* 48, p. 99.

that was a "romantic Trotskyist," not to be confused with the "realistic" Lenin who was only concerned with the "structure of organization." And probably his blueprint was intended for Britain or Germany, not for underdeveloped Russia.

There is nothing "utopian" in taxing only the rich peasants; several governments in the workers' states have tried to do precisely this, since the disastrous experience of Stalin's agricultural policy. The "realistic" Mao strongly insisted on policies of a similar kind. Even less is it "utopian" to try and reduce state expenditure (a huge part of which is wasted in most underdeveloped countries) by insisting on strict control of this expenditure from below and· by transferring a growing number of state functions to workers and peasants.[17] The proposals of the Left Opposition's program in that respect were worked out by some of the U.S.S.R.'s top economic specialists, among them Evgeny Preobrazhensky and Grigory Piatakov, who later actually built up Russia's heavy industry in the First Five-Year Plan. To accuse these experts of pandering to romantic daydreams is not very serious.

As a matter of fact, the figures quoted by the Left Opposition's platform dovetail with those that Krizhanovsky had worked out in his first comprehensive plan for industrializing the country in the early twenties. They also dovetail with what actually happened during the First Five-Year Plan.

The difference is that the sacrifice in consumption would have been spread over ten years, instead of being compressed into four-and-a-half years. It could thereby have been concentrated on the more privileged strata of the population instead of burdening especially workers and toiling peasants.

Its negative impact on the average productivity of labor (efficiency of investments) would have been negligible, whereas the impact of the concentrated sacrifices of those years on that productivity of labor was disastrous.

Finally, under the Left Opposition's program, waste and

---

[17] Cf. Lenin in his last article: "Better less but better." "We must reduce our state apparatus to the utmost degree of economy . . . only by thoroughly purging our government machine, by reducing to the utmost everything that is not absolutely essential in it, shall we be certain of being able to keep going." (*Collected Works,* Vol. 33, pp. 501–502).

losses would have been reduced, whereas they were increased tenfold under Stalin's "crash" industrialization plan when the disastrous lowering of efficiency of investments, resulting from the decline in real income of the producers, created the need for hundreds of thousands of supervisors and policemen busy "disciplining" the people and whose income was pure waste from the point of view of economic growth.

In this way, the tempo of economic growth, the level of consumption of the producers, and the degree of Soviet democracy are all interrelated, but in the opposite way many apologists for Stalinism generally assume (and Krassó seems to imply). More Soviet democracy and a higher immediate consumption of the producers strongly increase the productive effect of investments, reduce the need of much unproductive consumption, and make for a higher and not a lower rate of economic growth.

The time factor, which Krassó so conveniently eliminates from his argument, is vital indeed. It is also an answer to Krassó's rather absurd statement that Trotsky's alternative economic policy of 1923 was no answer to the kulaks blockading the towns in 1928. Of course it wasn't, because the whole point in that alternative policy was precisely to *prevent* a situation like that of 1928 from arising!

Trotsky and his comrades warned, as early as 1923, that growing differentiation in the countryside was an inevitable corollary of the growth of petty commodity production. He warned that this could lead to growing concentration of the marketable surplus of food in the hands of the rich peasants and to the growing weight of the rich peasants in the village, in the political field as well. Joseph Stalin and Nikolai Bukharin strenuously denied this. They alleged that it was the middle peasant who was being strengthened by the prosperity of petty commodity production, and not the rich peasant. They saw growing harmony where Trotsky predicted growing class struggle. They proposed to "integrate" private agriculture into the "building of socialism" to the point that expanded reproduction of socialist industry could be financed through . . . sale of state bonds to private peasants.

Trotsky rejected these utopian dreams of social harmony. He warned the party and the proletariat of the kulak danger years before that danger became acute. He actually predicted the exact form that danger would take: refusal to deliver food to the city as long as more industrial goods would not flow from the city to the village. He predicted the political showdown this "delivery strike" would provoke. And he had a realistic alternative policy to propose, as against the Stalin-Bukharin policy, which favored concentration of the food surplus in the hands of the kulaks. This alternative policy was: accelerated industrialization through taxing the kulaks on the one hand; and on the other, gradual collectivization of agriculture by building up state tractor factories and cooperative farms, based upon mechanized agriculture, into which poor peasants would gradually flock because their income and standard of life would from the start be higher in these farms than it was on the old miserable homestead.

Accelerated industrialization creating the basis for gradual mechanization of agriculture; accelerated differentiation of the peasantry not in favor, but at the expense, of the rich peasants; accelerated turn toward increased political activity of the poor in city and countryside, and therefore accelerated democratization —these were the consistent elements of Trotsky's program. Krassó can only state that this program "contains no political solution for the problem of the peasantry." No proof is advanced for this astonishing statement, and it cannot be accepted merely on the strength of Krassó's assertion, especially since facts and objective analysis point in the opposite direction.

The Nature of the Soviet Bureaucracy

When faced with the central social problem of the twenties in the Soviet Union, the problem of the bureaucracy, Krassó squirms and twists but cannot bring himself to recognize its *emergence as an autonomous social layer*. This is what prevents him from seeing the struggle inside the CPSU of that period on any other level than that of naked power politics and inadequate individual psychology.

Even Krassó's terminology is an indicator of this obstinate refusal to recognize a social problem. He speaks alternatively about "bureaucratism," "bureaucratic and administrative étatism," "bureaucratic and authoritarian tendencies." He even uses the absurd term "bureaucratic restoration" (whatever this may mean). Only once, and in direct quotation from my essay, does he use himself the obvious concept of "bureaucracy."

This is a direct imitation of the Stalinist habit of the twenties and thirties that was reborn in the post-Stalinist period of the late fifties. To utter laments about "bureaucratic habits" or "bureaucratic and étatist tendencies" is to hide a social problem behind observations on individual "habits" or "errors." Bureaucratism can assist the rise of a privileged bureaucracy; but it should not be confused with it. The appearance of a bureaucracy that tends to monopolize the exercise of political power, the administration of the social surplus product and, thence, to dominate all spheres of social life was recognized by Marx, as early as 1871, as a potential danger for the society emerging from the overthrow of capitalism. It was recognized in the same way by Kautsky and the anarchists in the 1890s. Lenin dwelt on it at length in all his writings after the beginning of the Russian Revolution of 1917.

> Lenin precisely never posed the problem idealistically, with the "either/or" of political romanticism. It was not for Lenin a question of bureaucracy or no bureaucracy. Lenin was acutely aware of the insurmountable contradictions that dominated both internal and external policy. . . . Lenin's aim was not the impossible one of complete triumph over bureaucratism; it was rather that he was looking for *correctives* to it.[18]

So far does Krassó go.

The bureaucracy arises out of the social division of labor, which has not yet been overcome, as a result of an insufficient level of development of the productive forces, an insufficient degree of technical and cultural skill of the working class. Therefore, it cannot be abolished by decrees any more than commodity production, money, or the state can be "abolished." All these phenomena can only wither away in the process of building a classless society. In that sense, it is ABC to state that it is not a question of "either bureaucracy or no bureaucracy." Complete and immediate suppression of bureaucracy (of all full-time paid state, party, and trade union functionaries; of all managers of the economy fulfilling these functions full-time, separate, and apart

---

[18] *New Left Review*, 48, p. 97.

from production workers; of all intellectuals divorced from productive labor, etc.) is impossible on the morrow of the victory of the socialist revolution. It is even more impossible in a backward country.

Trotsky knew this as well as Lenin. Nowhere, at no time, did he propose a plan for "immediate and total abolition of bureaucracy." But it is one thing to understand that bureaucracy is an inevitable *evil,* and quite another to make a virtue out of necessity. It is one thing to say: "We shall tolerate inequality only insofar as it helps us attain equality more quickly. In the meantime, we will not close our eyes to the corrupting influences of this inequality and will strive to reduce these by all means at our disposal." It is quite another thing to proclaim boldly that equality is a "petit-bourgeois ideal" and "realism" calls for robustly strengthening social inequality. It is one thing, in short, to allow a policy of gradually reducing the weight and power of the bureaucracy; it is another to increase its power and weight by leaps and bounds. The first is the attitude of proletarian revolutionists, from Lenin to Trotsky, the second is the attitude of spokesmen of the bureaucracy, from Stalin to Leonid Brezhnev.

To say that Lenin looked only for *correctives* to the power of bureaucracy is again a real slander of that great proletarian revolutionist. He was acutely aware of the tremendous danger that the growth of the bureaucracy represented for building a socialist society. While understanding that it was impossible to abolish that bureaucracy at one stroke, he strove with all his might to reduce its weight *as much as possible.* This is not a question of finding some subjective "correctives." It is a matter of finding both social forces and political processes and institutions that can prevent, within the limits of what was objectively possible, the bureaucratic deformation of the workers' state from becoming a bureaucratic degeneration, a cancer eating away the healthy parts of the organism.[19] And the objective force gradually able to reduce the

---

[19] Krassó dwells a lot on Lenin's capacity to make compromises. But Lenin made crystal clear that he accepted only those compromises that enabled a Communist party, "to raise—not lower—the general level of proletarian class-consciousness, revolutionary spirit, and ability to fight and win" (*Collected Works,* Vol. 31, p. 74). In the same "treatise on compromises" contained in his polemical article "Left-Wing Communism:

weight of the bureaucracy can only be the proletariat, by itself exercising more and more functions of direct administration of the state and of the economy.

Trotsky's attitude toward the problem of bureaucracy was in no way fundamentally different from that of Lenin. At no time did he nurse the illusion that bureaucracy could be "abolished" at one stroke. He attempted to reduce its growth and limit its nefarious effects upon Soviet society, to set into motion processes that would accelerate the withering away of that bureaucracy. If anything, he reacted slower than Lenin to the gravity of the danger, although he perceived earlier than Lenin the economic roots of the bureaucracy's power in addition to its social, political, and cultural roots.[20] But both Lenin and Trotsky understood the nature of the bureaucracy as a social layer and the absolute necessity to reduce its growth. The majority of the Old Bolsheviks didn't understand this problem at all. That was the ideological root of their own undoing.

Krassó only imitates their lack of understanding. Any idea that the *party* could neutralize the bureaucracy by itself is an illusion shared by the Old Bolsheviks. For under conditions of increasing passivity of the proletariat, the party inevitably became bureaucratized itself and thus a vehicle of bureaucratic power and not an obstacle to it.

Socialism in One Country

We explained at length in our "Trotsky: An Anti-Critique" in what respects Krassó's version of the debate around "so-

An Infantile Disorder" (1918), he makes no less clear that an inflexible resolution to fight opportunism should be combined with the necessity for making certain compromises. This resolution completely disappears from Krassó's analysis. What remains is the caricature of a Lenin willing to make "compromises" with the bureaucracy, at the price of not only lowering but crushing proletarian class consciousness and revolutionary spirit in the U.S.S.R.—a caricature indeed!

[20] In the trade union dispute, Trotsky, notwithstanding his incorrect overall position, understood in a clearer way than Lenin that the socio-economic roots of the power of the bureaucracy lie in its managing the economy and disposing of the social surplus product.

cialism in one country" and "permanent revolution" was inadequate, and how, up to this very day, Krassó doesn't seem to
understand what this discussion was all about: the ultimate and
final *conclusion* of the process of building a classless society, and
not at all the *beginning* of this process.

Krassó does not try to refute our analysis. He limits himself
to a few jibes about our "banalization" of the concept of permanent revolution. He argues, on the basis of two sentences quoted
from Trotsky's *Permanent Revolution* (1928), that Trotsky was
afraid of "an economic or military collapse of the U.S.S.R." [21]
This kind of polemics cannot be taken very seriously.

Krassó has not cited a single sentence of Trotsky's tending
to justify his preposterous interpretation of the theory of permanent revolution as implying the belief "in the imminence and
ubiquity of insurrection." We can, on the contrary, cite many
passages where Trotsky explicitly rejects infantile interpretations
like Krassó's. Here, for instance, is an answer to Bukharin,
written forty years ago, which reads like an anticipated answer to
Krassó:

> Naturally, I never shared the Bukharinist version of the
> theory of the "permanent" revolution, according to which no
> interruptions, periods of stagnation, retreats, transitional demands,
> or the like, are at all conceivable in the revolutionary process.
> On the contrary, from the first days of October, I fought against
> this caricature of the permanent revolution.
>
> When I spoke, as did Lenin, of the incompatibility between
> Soviet Russia and the world of imperialism, I had in mind the
> great strategical curve, and not its tactical windings. Bukharin,
> on the contrary, prior to his transformation into his own antipode,
> invariably expounded a scholastic caricature of the Marxian con-
> ception of a continuous revolution. Bukharin opined in the days
> of his "Left Communism" that the revolution allows neither of
> retreats nor temporary compromises with the enemy. Long after
> the question of the Brest-Litovsk Peace, in which my position
> had nothing in common with Bukharin's, the latter, together with
> the entire Ultra-Left wing of the Comintern of that time, advo-
> cated the line of the March 1921 days in Germany, being of the
> opinion that unless the proletariat in Europe was "galvanized,"
> unless there were ever new revolutionary eruptions, the Soviet

---

[21] *New Left Review*, 48, p. 98.

power was threatened with certain destruction. The consciousness that real danger actually threatened the Soviet power did not prevent me from waging an irreconcilable struggle shoulder to shoulder with Lenin at the Third Congress against this putschistic parody of a Marxian conception of the permanent revolution. During the Third Congress, we declared tens of times to the impatient Leftist: "Don't be in too great a hurry to save us. In that way you will only destroy yourselves and, therefore, also bring about our destruction. Follow systematically the path of the struggle for power. We need your victory but not your readiness to fight under unfavorable conditions. We will manage to maintain ourselves in the Soviet republic with the help of the NEP, and we will go forward. You will still have time to come to our aid at the right moment if you will have gathered your forces and will have utilized the favorable situations."[22]

These lines were written in June, 1928; Trotsky's pamphlet *The Permanent Revolution* was completed in October, 1928. Both documents are therefore virtually contemporary. However, Krassó, in the face of such striking documentary evidence, maintains his interpretation of Trotsky's theory of permanent revolution as identical with "Bukharin's caricature" of it, i.e., a conception of simultaneous and uninterrupted insurrection everywhere, which Trotsky rejects completely (in such a clear and explicit way).

The same can be said of Krassó's desperate attempt to uphold an interpretation of Trotsky's rejection of the "theory of socialism in one country" as implying the inevitability of the collapse of the Soviet regime, either through "the world market" or through foreign intervention, if world revolution is not rapidly victorious. Here again, let Trotsky speak for himself, in the introduction to *The Permanent Revolution:*

> A realistic program for an isolated workers' state cannot set itself the goal of achieving "independence" from world economy, much less of constructing a national socialist society "in the shortest time." The task is not to attain the abstract maximum tempo, but the optimum tempo, that is, the best, that which follows from both internal and world economic conditions, strengthens the position of the proletariat, prepares the national elements of the future international socialist society, and at the same time,

---

[22] Leon Trotsky: *The Third International After Lenin* (New York: Pioneer Publishers, 1936), pp. 88–89.

and above all, systematically improves the living standard of the proletariat and strengthens its alliance with the nonexploiting masses of the countryside. This prospect must remain in force for the whole preparatory period, that is, until the victorious revolution in the advanced countries liberates the Soviet Union from its present isolated position.[23]

There is not an atom of historical pessimism here, no foundation whatsoever of any conception of an "inevitable collapse" of the Soviet Union, maliciously attributed to Trotsky by his factional opponents and irresponsibly repeated by Krassó. There is understanding of the fact that there can only be temporary armistices in the class war, nationally and internationally, and not permanent "peaceful coexistence"; that the fundamental task of the world proletariat cannot be limited to that of "preventing" an international war of aggression against the Soviet Union, but that it must strive toward international extension of the revolution, or, in other words, that in the long run any grave defeat of the international working class—like Hitler's coming to power—makes such an international war of aggression more and more inevitable.

Here is the real *nexus* of the "theory of ultimately achieving the building of socialism in one country" and the basically conservative attitude of the Soviet bureaucracy toward world revolution. What the theory of "socialism in one country" implied was a strategic conception that considered the "defense of the bastion" the main task of the world revolutionary movement, and conceived of that "defense" as a subordination of the policies of national communist parties to the conjunctural twists and turns of Soviet diplomacy. The sad story, from the Anglo-Soviet Trade Union Council of 1925–26 to the policy of "peaceful coexistence" today, through the "Third Period," the turn toward "Popular Frontism," the sudden twist during the interlude of the Hitler-Stalin pact, the new turn after Hitler attacked the Soviet Union, the interlude of "Browderism," the turn toward the cold war and the Zhdanov period, the Cominform and its subsequent liquidation, is too well known to need detailed exposure or to be seriously challenged.

---

[23] Leon Trotsky, *The Permanent Revolution* (London: New Park Publications, 1962), p. 33.

What Trotsky contended, and what we contend, is that such a subordination of the policies of the national communist parties to the conjunctural needs of the Soviet diplomacy was detrimental *both* to the interests of the Soviet Union and to those of world revolution. It was surely not in the interests of the military defense of the Soviet Union that Chiang Kai-shek should be allowed to crush the Chinese workers' movement in 1927; that Hitler should come to power in Germany; that the French general strike of June, 1936, should end in nothing but a few economic reforms (and, incidentally, would lead to a return to power of conservative reaction less than two years later); that Franco should crush the Spanish revolution; that the working-class movement should be driven into the underground nearly everywhere in Europe.

Krassó lamely states: "Stalin's policies were not Furies, with power of life and death over the world revolutionary movement. They were cautious and conservative moves of the Soviet state." [24] But he suddenly forgets what he had written a few pages before on the nature of that state. Did this consistent "conservatism" reflect the interests of the Russian working class? If not, was it perhaps a reflection of the fact that the "bureaucratic deformation" of that workers' state had progressed beyond the wildest fears of Lenin in 1920–21? Where Krassó finds only *individual* psychology—Stalin's "caution and conservatism"—a Marxist of necessity looks for a *social* explanation.

The Comintern and World Revolution

Krassó takes strong exception to our contention that Stalin and the Soviet bureaucracy bear a heavy responsibility for the series of crushing defeats that world revolution suffered in the period 1923–43. He makes things easy for himself by knocking down a straw man he first erected: "The Kremlin becomes responsible for every suppression of social discontent and every victory of counterrevolution. This is a notion incompatible with any rational appreciation of world history." [25]

We did not make any such radical allegation; neither did

[24] *New Left Review*, 48, p. 102.
[25] *Ibid.*, p. 100.

Trotsky. To reduce all the factors whose interplay determine the course of world history to a single isolated one, and the role of a single individual at that, would be the antithesis of both vulgar and sophisticated Marxism (how it can be attributed to Trotsky *together* with his alleged "sociologism" is a contradiction Krassó doesn't try to explain). What we did contend, and what Trotsky, and Lenin before him, contended, is that if revolutionary situations exist, the role of the party, of party leadership, can be decisive. This certainly was so in Russia. Or does Krassó underestimate the "autonomous role of political institutions" to the point of presuming that the October Revolution would have won without a correct policy of the Bolshevik party?

To be sure, there were numerous instances in the international class struggle between 1923 and 1943 where obviously revolutionary situations did not come about. Even there, a correct policy of a revolutionary party could speed up the process of maturing its preconditions by helping to transform a prerevolutionary into a revolutionary situation. But let us dwell on those cases where revolutionary situations did exist or could be brought out into the open in a short-term perspective. We shall take up two examples that Krassó dismisses in too light-handed a way.

First, the Spanish revolution of July, 1936. Any study of the subject, which Krassó could undertake by reading not only half a dozen books, but especially the newspapers of that epoch, would teach him that in July, 1936, in reply to a military uprising of the fascist generals, the workers rose and broke the conspiracy almost bare-handedly in practically every major town of the country and in all the industrial centers in a few days time. They seized the barracks and the factories, armed themselves, and started to produce industrially—and also agriculturally on the large estates— on their own socialist basis.

For Krassó the question reduces itself to this "realistic" platitude: "Yet they (the Spanish Communists) were only a small minority of the Republican forces at the time, which themselves had little chance of winning the war once the military relationship of forces crystallized in 1936." [26] He doesn't even understand that he takes for granted what he has first to prove: to wit, that

---

[26] *Ibid.,* p. 101.

the "stabilization" or "crystallization" of the military relationship of forces was somehow predetermined (one would like to know by what!); that it was independent of the "crystallization" of social and political forces (among them, for example, a constant propaganda for radical agrarian revolution, and an immediate proclamation of independence of Spanish Morocco, which would have created powerful disintegrating trends among Franco's troops); that it was independent of the political orientation taken by the so-called People's Front government; and that the specific weight of Stalinism inside that government depended only on the two or three Stalinist cabinet ministers, and not upon the pressure of the Soviet Union, its limited deliveries of weapons to that government, and the tremendous power of blackmail that resulted from these deliveries.[27]

Of course, in the abstract, one could argue that if the Spanish working class had in fact reached a level of consciousness permitting it to build a revolutionary party independent of Moscow in time, Moscow's role could not have prevented a victorious revolution. Cuba's example is to the point here. But this is timeless abstract reasoning. The Spanish revolution broke out less than twenty years after the victory of the October Revolution. There was no reason for the working class, except a tiny vanguard, to doubt that the Stalin government was the continuator of the Soviet government that had created the Communist International in order to further the cause of world revolution. They therefore could not understand, until it was too late, the need to build another party to lead their revolution.

Stalin in turn abused this confidence and faith in the Soviet Union and the Communist International in order to strengthen his military alliance with imperialist France. Look here, gentlemen of the City and of the Paris Bourse, he said, I don't want to make trouble in your colonies; I don't want to make a socialist revolution in Spain; I am your faithful ally. This was the gist of his

---

[27] So strong was this pressure that it made the government, including anarchists and social democrats, not to speak of liberal bourgeois, accept tacitly the use of the GPU to abduct, torture, and murder revolutionists who favored a course toward socialist revolution, among them Andreas Nin who had been their colleague in the government of Catalonia a few months earlier.

Spanish policy. As a result of this, the small bourgeois and petit-bourgeois forces inside the Republican camp relied heavily on the Communist Party to do the counterrevolutionary job; it was more energetic and could disorient the workers more efficiently since it carried on this job of counterrevolution under the banner of the great Russian Revolution. When the Republican forces started to liquidate the revolutionary conquests of July, 1936, demoralization and defeat became inevitable. This is the real dialectic of social and political forces in Spain, in which Stalin played an important key role.[28]

A second example is the postwar policy of the French and Italian communist parties: the policy of liquidating the armed workers' formations created during the Resistance, of entering coalition governments, of bolstering up the bourgeois state and bourgeois economy, of even covering up for counterrevolutionary repressions and wars in the colonies (the huge bloodletting in Algeria in May, 1945, and the beginning of the war of aggression against Vietnam were undertaken while the French C.P. participated in the government). For Krassó, the question is very simple: the success of an armed bid for power in France or Italy was very problematic.[29] Here again he begs the question. We did not speak of an immediate armed bid for power. We spoke of a *strategy*

[28] It should be said in passing that the excuse cited at that time about the military threat of Nazi Germany has not at all been confirmed by historical sources now at our disposal. We know today that Germany in the summer of 1936 was only in the initial stage of its rearmament; that the U.S.A. and Britain were nearly completely disarmed; and that the strongest armies on the continent of Europe if not in the world were the Russian and French ones—with France on the threshold of revolution and with several million workers occupying their factories in June, 1936. This was indeed a turning point in history, and Krassó doesn't invoke facts but only a few abstractions to deny that a successful revolution in Spain, which a different Soviet policy would have made possible, could have changed the fate of Europe and halted Fascism's march toward dominating the whole continent.

[29] Be it said in passing, it is not true that the Left was stronger in Greece than in France or Italy in 1944–47. In France, communists and socialists had an absolute majority in the first elected Assembly. The weight of the proletariat was much greater in these countries than in Greece.

directed toward a victorious socialist revolution. Surely, when the Italian workers rose on July 14, 1948, to occupy a great number of strategic key centers in the country, it would not have been easy for "American troops" (how many remained there?) to crush an Italian revolution. Surely, if the C.P. had had an orientation toward a revolution from 1944 on, this uprising would have been much more powerful than it in fact was. Surely, the reformist policies of both the French and Italian communist parties in the 1944–48 period cannot be considered an insignificant factor in shaping the subsequent evolution of relationships of forces in the countries.

When the German revolution failed in 1919–20, all kinds of "explanations" could be found, each of which contained a grain of truth. Some even brought to bear upon this analysis the fact that serfdom was abolished in Prussia only at the beginning of the nineteenth century (conveniently forgetting that it was abolished in Russia more than half a century later, which did not prevent the revolution from being victorious there).

Lenin cut through all this underbrush of sophistication by laying the responsibility squarely at the feet of the social democrats. He thereby exhibited neither his "idealism" nor his "sociological monism." He only showed elementary revolutionary common sense: when a revolutionary situation comes about in a country whose working class for several decades had been following a party that claimed to be in favor of socialism, then, obviously, the policies of that party will have a heavy influence on the outcome of the revolution. It is very difficult to change the helmsman in the middle of the stream. If the social democratic helmsman bears heavy responsibility for the defeat in Germany in 1919–21, then the Stalinist helmsman bears a similar responsibility for a series of defeats in the thirties and the forties.

Krassó argues that Trotsky underestimated the *national* framework of the class struggle. Ironically, this is in reality precisely what Stalin did in the interests of the Soviet bureaucracy's diplomacy. In all countries, communist parties had to apply the same tactics mechanically (i.e., the Indian C.P.'s opposition to the national uprising of July, 1942), strictly governed by conjunctural twists of the Soviet bureaucracy. Trotsky, on the other hand, urged that the Comintern and the Soviet state should not interfere with the needs of the revolutionary class struggle, as they developed in each country, but should assist the C.P.'s to conquer the majority of the exploited masses in these countries, and eventually to conquer power. Whereas this strategy was the most efficient defense of the Soviet Union in the long run, it also demanded a scrupulous and objective analysis of the social and political relationship of forces in each particular country at each particular moment. To picture Trotsky as a man who wanted "insurrection" always and everywhere is to repeat a typical Stalinist slander.

The Unity of Theory and Practice

In " 'Trotsky's Marxism': An Anti-Critique," we made the point that, after trying to counterpose Lenin systematically to Trotsky, Krassó's critique of Trotsky's theory and practice after 1923 objectively leads to a revision of Lenin's basic theory and practice. It is hard to challenge Trotsky consistently without challenging Lenin—if only because Trotsky was the most consistent defender and continuator of Leninism after 1923.

Krassó admits that Trotsky was right in his industrialization proposals. He admits he was right in his criticism of the Comintern's policies in Germany in 1930–33.[30] If we take only these two points of Trotsky's struggle, we are already faced with formidable consequences. It is absurd to assert that on these issues Trotsky was guided by "beatific optimism"; the opposite is true. He was guided by the urge to head off an approaching catastrophe. In Russia, the very existence of Soviet power was at stake; in Germany, the existence of the strongest working-class movement in the West, if not that of the whole European working-class movement, was threatened.

Let us confront Krassó with a simple question: what should

---

[30] It is not accidental that Krassó only approves Trotsky's criticisms against the ultraleft policies of the Comintern; his attitude toward right-wing opportunism is ambiguous, to say the least. But how can one claim to take Lenin as a model and, at the same time, wipe the slate clean of Lenin's consistent and ferocious struggle against right-wing opportunism?

Trotsky have done in these two specific situations? Keep quiet? Limit his criticism to inner-party statements? And what if these were suppressed, as they were after 1926? Should he have satisfied himself with the confidence—beatific optimism!—that the party would somehow, sometime, "correct its course," independently of the social forces that were bearing down upon it, independently of its internal regime, which called upon the Left Opposition to abandon its opinion independently of the objective consequences of their own mistakes? Or should he have withdrawn to the position of a "critical observer" of the world scene, limiting himself to the kibitzer's remarks of an outsider, unwilling or unable to descend into the arena of actual struggle?

Krassó will have a hard time convincing anybody that these two possible alternatives to Trotsky's course—either conciliation with opportunism or withdrawal from practical politics—represent "Leninism" in any sense whatsoever! In the whole history of Lenin's activity as a political leader, he will be unable to cite a single instance of such an attitude on his part. Whenever Lenin thought that the party majority was wrong, he fought against those wrong ideas with an energy and singleness of purpose even greater than that of Trotsky after 1923. This was true before the conquest of power; it remained true after the conquest of power (the full scope of his final struggle against Joseph Stalin and Grigory Ordzhonikidze in the Georgian question has only recently become known, since the publication of the now-famous Volume 36 of his *Complete Works*). It is unthinkable to suppose that Lenin would have conciliated with the bureaucracy or capitulated before it; it is even more unthinkable that he would have withdrawn from political activity altogether.

Krassó could argue that, with Lenin alive, the bureaucracy could have been defeated as early as 1923. But this again runs away from the real problem. It is difficult to argue, at one and the same time, that the working class was nearly "disintegrated" at that moment and that the reaffirmation of its power would have been a simple question of one leader (Lenin) acting more efficiently than another (Trotsky). The inability of the Old Guard to recognize and readjust to a sharp turn of events was not something new. It had occurred before in February–March, 1917. At that time Lenin could correct the wrong orientation through his "April Theses," because he could bank on the crest of a tremendous revolutionary upheaval, and thousands of Bolshevik workers clamored for the same turn that he demanded. In 1923–24, these workers were silent or dead. It is improbable, to say the least, that he could have reversed the bureaucratization of the party. The Old Guard was finished as a revolutionary instrument.

We have a clear precedent of how Lenin behaved when he thought that "the old party" had betrayed the socialist revolution in his attitude toward the Second International in 1914. His break was radical and ruthless. Numbers didn't count, nor did immediate mass influence. What counted was the program, correct ideas, expression of the historic interests of the working class. Lenin was absolutely confident that sooner or later the masses would turn toward the tiny internationalist minorities because social contradictions would sharpen and lead to new revolutionary upheavals. Up to now, history has confirmed this prognosis only partially, and only in certain countries. Does Krassó, admirer of the accomplished fact, then conclude that Lenin was wrong to break with the Second International and to call upon the internationalists to build new communist parties (which, in many cases, have remained small minorities to this very day)?

Trotsky followed the example of Lenin when he was confronted with the problem of the degeneration of the Soviet state and the Communist International. Neither conciliation with the bureaucratic opportunists nor withdrawal from revolutionary politics is acceptable to a Marxist. The unity of theory and practice demands that a historical turn of the international class struggle be met by a struggle for a new program that can only be embodied in a new organization, nationally and internationally. Like the call for the Third International by Lenin in 1914, the call for the Fourth International by Trotsky was produced by historic defeats in the class struggle. Like the call for the Third International, the call for the Fourth International was an act of confidence in the eventual new rise of world revolution.

Krassó tries to avoid answering these basic questions by taking two detours. He argues that power was indeed conquered in some countries by the proletariat under Communist Party leadership; he argues that Trotsky's Fourth International has remained impotent. On the first point, it is sufficient to remind Krassó that Trotsky did not exclude such an eventuality; [31] he only doubted that it would be the rule instead of remaining an exception. History has proved him right, and it has especially confirmed that in no industrialized country has the working class been able to take power without a revolutionary party trained in the correct Leninist program, strategy, and tactics.

On the second question, Krassó should be a bit more cautious. The ups and downs of the Bolshevik party are intertwined with the ups and downs of the revolution itself. In a period of reaction, Bolshevism is reduced to attempts to preserve the program, the continuity of theory, and the key cadre. In Russia it faced five years of reaction between 1907 and 1912; on a world scale, the Leninists faced twenty years of reaction, 1923–43. The effort to preserve the continuity of the program and the cadre was immeasurably more difficult because the period of reaction was much longer, the forms of reaction much more vicious—Fascism and Stalinism—and not the least because the attempt to build up the revolutionary movement had to be made for the third time on a world scale, after two attempts had failed, meeting much more skepticism on the part of the proletariat.

This period of reaction was followed by a period of upsurge which, after a few years' interlude, was confined almost exclusively to the more backward parts of the world, where neither the programmatic nor the social preconditions for a rebirth of Leninism were very favorable. But once the tide of world revolution turns toward the countries with a huge industrial proletariat, the situation changes radically. France and Czechoslovakia, in 1968, have proven convincingly that revolution cannot return to the West without reasserting the basic aspects of Leninism: revolutionary class struggle, soviet-type state power, proletarian internationalism. The Fourth International happens to be the only

---

[31] *Transitional Program of the Fourth International,* drafted by Trotsky, in the 1930s, states explicitly that one cannot exclude that, under exceptional circumstances of war and disintegration of the old social order, the opportunist working-class parties could be compelled through the pressure of the masses to take the road to power. This is exactly what happened in the cases cited by Krassó.

organization that today embodies these programmatic foundations in living cadres and nuclei of organizations on the five continents. It is living Leninism today.

We can now oppose to Krassó's definition of "Trotsky's Marxism" a more adequate one. Trotsky's Marxism is an attempt at incorporating into the classic tenets of scientific socialism an answer to the specific problems of the imperialist epoch of revolutions and counterrevolutions: the problem of soviet power [32] as the basis for the dictatorship of the proletariat; the problem of permanent revolution in the backward countries; the problem of the international dynamic of a victorious proletarian revolution; the problem of the dual nature of working-class bureaucracy; the problem of the relationship between party, party apparatus, and the class. His very weaknesses—like his belated understanding of the need of a Bolshevik party and its key role in the historic process of proletarian revolution—are an expression of this gigantic effort. Parts of that answer became integrated into classical Marxism as early as 1917. Others became progressively integrated into revolutionary Marxism after 1923.

Trotsky's Marxism is an attempt to assert the proletarian nature of the revolutionary doctrine, under the triple onslaught of petit-bourgeois opportunism, nationalism, and the threat of bureaucratic regeneration. It is an attempt to bring the Marxist understanding of history to its highest level, through the discovery and application of the law of uneven and combined development. No victory of world revolution is possible today without the assimilation of the main elements of Trotsky's Marxism.

Empiricism and Marxist Historiography: A Second Approach

Our definition of Trotsky's Marxism, as opposed to Krassó's, hinges on two basic pivots: the appraisal of the historic nature of

---

[32] Trotsky was the first to understand theoretically the key role of the *soviet* as the basis for organizing a new proletarian state apparatus. Lenin incorporated this concept into recognized Bolshevik theory only in 1917, as he incorporated it in 1919–20 into the programmatic documents of the Communist International.

the epoch opened up by the October Revolution; and the appraisal of the social background of the debate and struggle in the world communist movement since 1923. We define that epoch as the epoch of world revolution (which implies, of course, many relapses into counterrevolution); we define this struggle as a basic struggle between the Soviet bureaucracy and the working class. In the framework of this explanation, Trotsky represented the historic interests of the Soviet state and the international proletariat by fighting against the bureaucratic degeneration of the Soviet state and the Communist International.

Now confront this explanation with Krassó's summing up of his position:

> Trotsky's indifferences to political institutions divided him from Lenin before the October Revolution, and excluded him from the Bolshevik party. His previous theory and practice then isolated him within the party in the twenties, and ultimately ensured his defeat. In the thirties, his abstract internationalism prevented him from understanding the complex intranational dynamics that governed the main development of the different detachments of the world revolutionary movement.[33]

This judgment implies two basic revisions of Marxism. A historic political struggle, involving hundreds of thousands of people and having the most far-reaching consequences for the international class struggle, is explained by the juvenile mistakes of a single person. A confrontation of even more gigantic proportions, involving the discontent, protest, and potential revolt of tens of millions of manual and intellectual workers against the bureaucracy, is reduced to that pious platitude: "complex intranational dynamics that governed the main development of the different detachments of the world revolutionary movement." It would be very hard for Krassó to explain to the survivors of the forced labor camps in Siberia, not to speak of the Hungarian workers of 1956 or the Czech workers of 1968, that what clamped down on them was not a conservative bureaucracy trying to defend its power and privileges, but "complex intranational dynamics."

Krassó's attempt to divorce his interpretation of Trotsky's

---

[33] *New Left Review,* 48, p. 103.

Marxism from the living dialectics of social forces and their struggles does not make sense in a Marxist framework. It leads to crass empiricism in the evaluation of historical trends. It makes impossible a global appreciation of the era of world history opened by World War I. It leads necessarily to a complete reappraisal and revision of what Leninism stands for in the international field—especially for the founding of the Third International. And it leads to that final failure of anybody claiming to make an attempt at Marxist historiography: the confusion between subjective self-rationalization of individuals and groups and an appraisal of their objective role in history.

Krassó writes: "Trotsky was viewed, not as an ally, but as the main threat by the other Bolshevik leaders because of his non-Leninist past, because of his military supremacy, because of his authoritarian role during War Communism, and because of his commandism in the trade union debate." [34] In other words: Trotsky's mistakes in his youth (his authoritarian role during War Communism and his commandism in the trade union debate are largely myths) explain why he couldn't unite the Old Guard around himself.

We will not deny that this was certainly part of the rationalization by which Grigory Zinoviev and Nikolai Bukharin justified to themselves their ganging up with Stalin against Trotsky. But surely Krassó cannot be naïve to the point of identifying the social motives of political behavior with individual rationalizations of these motives in the heads of the actors of history's drama.

Marx long ago taught us not to judge people by what they say about themselves but by what they do. An individually honest social democrat in Germany could explain in December, 1918, that he was against a Soviet republic in his country because he was repelled by "red terror," Lenin's repression of the right-wing Mensheviks, his desire to defend democratic freedoms, his fear lest revolution produce counterrevolution, his conviction that "objective conditions were not ripe," etc., etc. But no Marxist (not to speak of a Leninist) will believe that these rationalizations actually *caused* his ganging up with the Reichswehr against "Sparatakus," which initiated the historical process eventually leading to Hitler's conquest of power and to the very same social

_____
[34] *Ibid.*, p. 93.

democrats finding themselves in concentration camps side by side with the communists.

The objective meaning of the German Social Democrats' attitude in 1919 was the alliance of a privileged workers' bureaucracy with bourgeois counterrevolution against the proletarian revolution. The basic theoretical reflection of this alliance was the lack of understanding of the problem of proletarian democracy as opposed to bourgeois democracy. The objective meaning of the Old Guard joining Stalin against Trotsky was their alignment with the Soviet bureaucracy against the Soviet proletariat. The basic theoretical reflection of this alignment was their lack of understanding of the problem of Soviet democracy versus bureaucratic dictatorship, as well as the lack of understanding of the theory of permanent revolution. All the rest is self-rationalization, important for understanding the mechanics of why and how certain individuals expressed certain social needs, but certainly not decisive for evaluating the social forces with which they aligned themselves.

Krassó is unable to interpret Trotsky's Marxism coherently because he tries to explain Trotsky's role in history by a few preconceived abstract "sins." He should ponder on Marx's opinion of Ferdinand Lassalle: "He (Lassalle) will learn to his cost that to bring a science by criticism to the point where it can be dialectically presented is an altogether different thing from applying an abstract ready-made system of logic to mere inklings of such a system." [35] This applies equally well to Krassó's misbegotten attempt to bring up to date the Marxist interpretation of the destinies of the Russian Revolution.

---

[35] Letter of Marx to Engels of February 1, 1858, in *Selected Correspondence*, p. 102.

ROBERTO JEPPE

A Comment on Krassó

Krassó's location of Trotsky's "sociologism" as the source of his weaknesses represents a considerable advance in the study of this passionate revolutionary. Trotsky's shortcomings in his analysis of the Chinese revolution illustrate this vividly. But Krassó's dictum that Trotsky had "the virtues of his vices" is mere dialectical rhetoric. We are told that when he was first to return to Russia in 1905 and became the major revolutionary agitator in St. Petersburg, this was because he represented *par excellence* the nonparty man. Does this also explain why he arrived after Lenin in 1917? How can his theses on "permanent revolution" prior to October, with all the lucidity contained in them, be explained by his "vices"? Perhaps Lenin's vices were all the greater, considering his indisputably greater virtues. . . .

These are minor points, of course. The central defect of Krassó's articles is their treatment of revolutions that failed. He may have a strong case with the British general strike of 1926. But what about France and Italy? Was failure in these countries solely due to a "problematic" political situation there? Was the defeat of the Greek revolution only caused by "Anglo-American invasion," as Krassó states? The Vietnamese would be in a very bad way if this were an insuperable obstacle to revolutions: or do the Vietnamese victories at Saigon or the Cuban victories at Playa Giron lack "consistent unity"?

It is true that Krassó's prejudices are not against revolutions, but only against those which fail: he writes of the Chinese revolution with esteem. But even this I find insulting. Can any unbiased person claim innocence of the political leadership in the defeat of the Greek revolution, the Filipino, or many others? Were these factors foreign to social conditions, existing in a fateful, autonomous empyrean of their own? Surely material facts exist, whatever they are, and we interpret and act on them in different ways—properly or improperly. In the case of the Communist International, everybody today agrees that there was a strong influence of the center, which in time acquired an undue and aberrant character. Some folded to it and some did not. Others respected the rhetoric, perhaps because they believed in it in a way, and made the revolution. Praise to them: Mao. But those who did not give in have at least the right to some merit. Those who merely obeyed had value only prior to their genuflections. Will Krassó argue that they were right in spite of them? Their virtues for their vices. I, as a Cuban, do not have so much flexibility. The chain of officialdom in the "churches of the left" of Latin America today is eloquent. Against them is an example where temporary failure overtook correct leadership: "Che" Guevara in Bolivia. Did the stroke of good luck of an inefficient, corrupt, and murderous military clique there convince Krassó of another impossibility? He writes of the small numbers of the Spanish Communist Party in 1936. Should I remind him that Fulgencio Batista always contended that Fidel Castro's rebels represented nobody because they were a few hundreds and the Cuban nation was seven million?

I consider all these status quo judgments on revolutions that failed as pernicious and unrepresentative of a journal that can offer an article like Göran Therborn's "From Petrograd to Saigon" in the same issue. This is not to deprecate the importance of Krassó's intellectual effort to clarify Trotsky's words and deeds: a new and sophisticated appraisal of Trotsky is undoubtedly needed.

NICOLAS KRASSÓ

Reply to Roberto Jeppe

1. By saying that Trotsky had the virtues of his vices I did not, of course, say that all his virtues were due to his vices.

2. As I wrote in my reply to Ernest Mandel:

> . . . the fact is that the Comintern did not in the last instance determine the fate of the revolutionary movements of every country in the world. . . . The vulgar anticommunist conviction that the "Kremlin" was responsible for every eruption of social discontent or revolution anywhere in the world here finds its vulgar Marxist opposite: the Kremlin becomes responsible for every suppression of social discontent and every victory of counterrevolution.

And:

> Those parties with enough vitality to ignore Comintern advice were those that had enough combative power to win the revolution. Those that docilely complied with mistaken directives of the Comintern were not those likely to rout the bourgeoisie.

But it is true that while docility toward Moscow was due to the weakness of the movements in question, the consequence of this docility—Comintern interference—led to further weakening and degeneration. This was a vicious circle. And Roberto Jeppe is right in stressing the overcentralized nature of the Comintern (which in any case came more and more to be a bureaucratic appendix of Russian foreign policy).

When I wrote of certain situations being "problematic" from the revolutionary point of view, I was not denying that Moscow policy was often an important negative factor, but just pointing out that *one* factor should not be isolated, absolutized, and made out to be more decisive than it actually was. Moreover, I stated quite unambiguously:

> Of course, Stalin's policies were wrong in France, Italy and, above all, Germany. I emphasized in my original essay the successive blunders of the Third International. Moreover, Trotsky's critique of the Comintern policies in Germany was excellent.

There would not be much point in going into details here, into the differences between the Vietnamese and Greek situations, etc. (The Stalin-Churchill "spheres of influence" agreement was of course a very important factor as far as Greece was concerned). I agree with Roberto Jeppe: our attitudes toward movements of the past should not be determined by the mere fact of their failure or success. Trotsky's attitudes were often voluntaristic and romantic—but his outlook (*Victrix causa diis placuit, sed victa Catoni*) was still vastly superior to the philistinism of the status quo outlook. I think that Roberto Jeppe is wrong in attributing the latter outlook to my essays.

MONTY JOHNSTONE

Socialism in One Country

The object of the present essay is to examine one area of the debate recently engaged in between Nicolas Krassó and Ernest Mandel—the question of "socialism in one country." This great historical controversy, waged from the outset in somewhat elusive terms and encrusted today with decades of polemical distortions by both sides, is one where it is particularly important to make an objective and balanced estimate of Trotsky's position, without any ideological or psychological disposition to "vindicate" one side as against the other.

A serious examination of what Trotsky actually said about building socialism in Russia reveals a fundamental and unresolved contradiction in his position, which does not appear in Mandel's bowdlerized version of it. On the one hand, as Mandel correctly states, Trotsky never disputed the need to *start* the job of building socialism, and advanced proposals for an increased rate of economic growth to this end.[1] Under attack, he denied

---

[1] I cannot in the scope of this article examine the question of how far Trotsky's proposals in 1923–24 for the introduction of central planning, and in 1925–27 for industrialization, corresponded to the real possibilities

having a "pessimistic attitude toward the program of our work of socialist construction in the face of the retarded process of revolution in the West," and accepted that "in spite of all the difficulties arising out of our capitalistic environment, the economic and political resources of the Soviet dictatorship are very great." [2] On the other hand he remained tied to the "fundamental proposition in the theory of permanent revolution" that the only "way out of those contradictions that will befall the proletarian dictatorship in a backward country, surrounded by a world of capitalist enemies, will be found on the arena of world revolution." [3]

Krassó is right in showing that the primary basis of Trotsky's argument against the possibility of completing the building of socialism in the Soviet Union was his disbelief in its ability even to survive as a workers' state if the revolution did not spread to more advanced countries. Since Mandel not only does not acknowledge the truth of this, but speaks darkly of "historical distortions" in Krassó's presentation (*New Left Review,* 47, p. 42), it would perhaps be useful to let Trotsky speak for himself—not in incidental and untypical quotations taken from their context, but in statements that represent the main content of his thinking on this question.

"Without the direct state support of the European proletariat, the working class of Russia cannot remain in power and convert its temporary domination into a lasting socialistic dictator-

---

existing at the time they were advanced. It is one of the myths of vulgar Trotskyism that the implementation by Stalin after 1928 of more far-reaching plans than had been put forward by the Opposition proves per se that the latter were correct. As Maurice Dobb writes: "it does not follow that what may have been practicable in 1928–29 was necessarily practicable at an earlier date when both industry and agriculture were weaker." (M. Dobb, *Soviet Economic Development Since 1917* [London, 1948], pp. 206–207.) See also, R. W. Davies, "The Inadequacies of Russian Trotskyism," in *Labour Review* (London), July–August, 1957. However, I would accept the argument that if the party had heeded earlier the Opposition's warnings against the dangerous growth in the power of the kulaks in the countryside, the process of collectivization in 1929–30 could have been less violent.

[2] Leon Trotsky, Letter to Plenum of C.C. of R.C.P., January 15, 1925, in J. Murphy (ed.), *Errors of Trotskyism* (London, 1925), p. 374.

[3] L. Trotsky, *The Third International After Lenin* (New York: Pioneer Publishers, 1957), p. 40.

ship," Trotsky wrote in 1906.[4] He vigorously defended this formulation in 1928 against criticism from Karl Radek, who had argued that in talking of state support Trotsky had excessively sharpened the presentation of the Soviet Union's undoubted need for aid from the workers of other countries.[5]

In 1915, in an article included two years later in his pamphlet *The Program of Peace,* which was republished with a postscript in 1922 and 1924, he wrote of the socialist revolution in Russia:

> Without waiting for the others we begin and we continue the struggle on our own national soil in complete certainty that our initiative will provide the impulse for the struggle in other countries; and if this were not so, then it would be hopeless to think— as is born out both by historical experience and theoretical considerations—that revolutionary Russia, for example, would be able to maintain herself in the face of conservative Europe, or that socialist Germany could remain isolated in a capitalist world.[6]

Outlining the theory of permanent revolution in a preface, written in 1922 (and unreservedly defended in 1928), to his book *1905,* he spoke of the proletarian vanguard in the early stages of its rule making deep inroads into capitalist property.

> In this it will come into hostile collision not only with all the groupings of the bourgeoisie which supported it in the first stages of its revolutionary struggle, but also with the broad masses of the peasantry with the help of which it came to power. The contradictions in the position of a workers' government in a backward country with a peasant majority can be solved only on an international scale on the arena of the world proletarian revolution.[7]

In 1937 the theme is essentially the same:

> *Without a more or less rapid victory of the proletariat in the advanced countries,* the workers' government in Russia will not survive. Left to itself, the Soviet regime must either fall or de-

---

[4] L. Trotsky, *Permanent Revolution* and *Results and Prospects* (New York, 1965), p. 237. Italics in original.

[5] *Ibid.,* pp. 138 ff.

[6] L. Trotsky, *The Program of Peace* (Colombo, 1956), p. 18.

[7] L. Trotsky, *1905* (Moscow, 1922), p. 4.

generate. More exactly it will first degenerate and then fall. I myself have written about this more than once, beginning in 1905.[8]

Economic Growth Underestimated

Trotsky's underestimation of the internal forces of Russian socialism was particularly evident in his lack of confidence in the independent development of a socialist economy in the U.S.S.R. In his 1922 Postscript to his *Program of Peace* he wrote:

> Socialism is conceivable only on the basis of the productive forces' growth and blossoming. . . . So long as the bourgeoisie remains in power in other European states we are compelled, in the struggle against economic isolation, to seek agreements with the capitalist world; at the same time it can be stated with certainty that these agreements, in the best case, will help us to heal this or that economic wound, make this or that step forward, but the genuine rise of socialist economy in Russia will become possible only after the victory of the proletariat in the most important countries of Europe.[9]

In 1927, we find him asserting that the Soviet state was

> always, directly or indirectly, under the relative control of the world market. Herein lies the root of the question. The rate of development is not an arbitrary one; it is determined by the whole of world development, because in the last analysis world industry controls every one of its parts, even if that part is under the proletarian dictatorship and is building up socialist industry.[10]

In his criticism of the *Draft Program of the Comintern* the next year he went even further:

> To the extent that productivity of labor and the productivity of a social system as a whole are measured on the market by the correlation of prices, it is not so much military intervention as

---

[8] L. Trotsky, *Stalinism and Bolshevism* (London, 1956), p. 9. Italics in original.

[9] L. Trotsky, *The Program of Peace*, pp. 20–21.

[10] *Where Is Trotsky Going?* (London, 1928), pp. 53–54.

the intervention of cheaper capitalist commodities that constitutes perhaps the greatest immediate menace to Soviet economy.[11]

There is thus no justification for Mandel's denial that Trotsky ever spoke of the planned economy of the U.S.S.R. being subverted by the capitalist world market. The monopoly of foreign trade, which Stalin and the party majority correctly stressed was the means of the Soviet Union to shield itself from such economic subversion, became for Trotsky "evidence of the severity and the dangerous character of our dependence." [12] He saw the fate of the world economy as a whole as of "decisive significance" as against the subsidiary significance of Russia's socialist construction.[13] He went on with the utmost defeatism to suggest the possibility of the productivity of labor growing faster in the predominant capitalist countries than in Russia.[14]

The fiasco of this approach was proved by the successes of the Soviet Five-Year Plans. Old revolutionary that he was, Trotsky could scarce forbear to cheer in 1936 when he viewed "the vast scope of industrialization in the Soviet Union, as against a background of stagnation and decline in almost all the capitalist world" that emerged from the comparative indices of industrial production.[15] But while noting that "it is impossible to deny the fact that even now the forces of production in the Soviet Union are developing at a tempo such as no other country in the world has ever experienced or is experiencing now," [16] he was never to admit that this was a direct refutation of his pessimistic predictions of the late twenties, which in their turn contrasted strangely with the superindustrialization proposals he had advanced at an earlier period. (It is the latter that are always pointed to by Trotsky's

---

[11] L. Trotsky, *The Third International After Lenin*, p. 47.

[12] *Ibid.*, p. 49. In a recent booklet, Ernest Germain of the Fourth International ridicules those who nowadays use just such arguments as did Trotsky about the Soviet Union's "subordination" to the world market—and refers them to the efficacy of . . . the monopoly of foreign trade! (E. Germain, *Marxism v. Ultra-Leftism* [Paris, 1967], pp. 69 ff.)

[13] L. Trotsky, *loc. cit.*

[14] *Ibid.*

[15] L. Trotsky, *The Revolution Betrayed* (New York, 1957), pp. 6 ff.

[16] L. Trotsky, in *Workers International News* (London), July 1938, p. 1.

defenders nowadays, while the former are conveniently forgotten.) Least of all was he to attempt a Marxist analysis of the source of his errors—a practice that he was always most ready to demand of his political adversaries. Rather, he was to draw the strange conclusion that these successes, though signifying that "the technical premise for socialism has made an enormous stride forward," were not leading Soviet society toward socialism but in the direction of "the regeneration of classes, the liquidation of planned economy and the restoration of capitalist property," in which case, he added, "the state will inevitably become fascist." [17]

A Question for Scholiasts?

Isaac Deutscher likened the logic of the argument over socialism in one country in the twenties to a dispute about whether it would be possible to cover with a roof a building on which both sides were in favor of starting work, already being in agreement on its shape and the materials to be used.[18] Isolated from the undercurrents expressing differences of mood and emphasis that lay behind the heat that it generated, such a debate appears highly scholastic. Apparently conscious of this, the *New International,* the leading American Trotskyist organ of the thirties (praised by Trotsky for its high theoretical level), openly expressed the essence of the Trotskyist position as follows in an editorial dated January 30, 1935:

> In the light of the present world situation, the theory of "socialism in one country," this gospel of the bureaucracy, stands before us in all its nationalistic limitation and its braggart falsity. We refer here, of course, not to the purely abstract possibility or impossibility of building a socialist society within this or another geographic area—such a theme is for scholiasts; we have in mind the vastly more immediate and concrete, living and historical, and not metaphysical question: is it possible for an isolated Soviet state to maintain itself for an indeterminate period of time in

---

[17] *Ibid.*, p. 2.
[18] Isaac Deutscher, *Stalin: A Political Biography* (London, 1949), pp. 286–287.

an imperialist environment, within the constricting circle of fascist counterrevolutions? The answer of Marxism is: No. The answer of the internal condition of the U.S.S.R. is: No! . . . Outside of the world revolution there is no salvation.[19]

If we accept the issue posed in this way, history has completely demolished Trotsky's position. If, however, we define socialism as Mandel does, as "a society without classes, commodities, money, and state," then by the very terms of this definition we are led to a different conclusion. If we are going to make a meaningful estimate of Trotsky's political positions, we must avoid arbitrary definitions that take the issues out of their historical context and provoke idle semantic wrangles. The fact is that Mandel's definition is at variance with the Leninist conception that was generally accepted by the Russian Communist Party. In *State and Revolution* Lenin wrote of socialism as synonymous with Marx's first phase of communism, representing the "conversion of the means of production into the common property of the whole of society." "Socialism," he went on, *"does not remove* the defects of distribution and the inequality of 'bourgeois right' which *continue to prevail* as long as the products are divided 'according to the amount of work performed. . . .' The socialist principle: 'An equal amount of labor for an equal quantity of products,' is . . . already realized. . . . There is still need for a state. . . . For the complete withering away of the state, complete communism is necessary." [20] This distinction was amplified in *The ABC of Communism,* by Nikolai Bukharin and Evgeny Preobrazhensky, which from 1919 had been the basic party textbook. "In socialist society, which is inevitable as an intermediate stage between capitalism and communism," they wrote, "money is needed, for it has a part to play in commodity economy. . . . In socialist society, this commodity economy will to some extent persist." [21] The society without commodities, money, and state, which Mandel defines as socialism, carries many of the characteristics that party tradition identified with the higher stage

[19] *New International* (New York), March, 1935, p. 40.

[20] V. I. Lenin, *Selected Works,* VII (Moscow, 1937), pp. 85–87. Italics in original. Cf. also VIII, p. 239.

[21] Nikolai Bukharin and Evgeny Preobrazhensky, *The ABC of Communism* (London, 1924), pp. 345–346.

of communism. It is a red herring drawn into the discussion, for it is not what Russian Communists understood when they set themselves the goal of creating a socialist economy—by which they meant the organization of "co-operative production on a large scale," to use the definition that Trotsky gave of socialism in 1906.[22]

Nor will Mandel be able to find any support for his claim that "even Stalin and Bukharin" agreed that the socialist economy that they believed possible in Russia "must have a higher productivity of labor than the most developed capitalist economy" —as distinct from a far higher level of productivity than Russia had known under capitalism and the aim of catching up with and overtaking the capitalist world in productivity—the guarantee of the victory of socialism *on a world scale.*[23]

Lenin's Position

Mandel argues that the conception of "socialism in one country" represents a rejection of elementary Marxist-Leninist theory, of "the whole heritage of Lenin." This is a particularly misleading quarter-truth. What is true is that when the Bolsheviks came to power in 1917, they did so in the belief that they were, in Lenin's words, "on the threshold of a world proletarian revolution." [24] For some time after the October Revolution, Lenin and the Bolsheviks thought (and Trotsky was very fond of marshaling quotations to prove it [25]): "Either revolution breaks out in the other countries, in the capitalistically more developed countries, immediately, or at least very quickly, or we must perish." [26] However, with characteristic realism, Lenin noted already in March, 1918—urging ratification of the humiliating terms of the Brest-Litovsk Peace Treaty that Trotsky said

---

[22] L. Trotsky, *Results and Prospects,* p. 220.

[23] Actually the average productivity of labor in the U.S.S.R. today is equal to and even above that of most capitalist countries, while being still below that of the U.S.A.

[24] *Selected Works,* VI, p. 225.

[25] See, e.g., L. Trotsky, *History of the Russian Revolution,* III (London, 1936), Appendix I.

[26] *Selected Works,* IX, p. 227.

would be "treachery in the fullest sense of the word" [27]—that although they eventually would see the world revolution, "for the time being it is a very good fairy tale." [28] Since by 1921 it was clear to him that internationally "events did not proceed along as straight a line as we expected" and it had "proved impossible to call forth revolution in other capitalist countries," [29] he devoted himself more and more to considering the novel problem of the construction of socialism in Russia in the context of an indefinitely delayed international revolution. On March 15, 1921, he had stressed two conditions on which the socialist revolution could be "completely successful" in Russia: first, that "it receives timely support from the socialist revolution in one or several advanced countries" and, second, that "the agreement between the proletariat . . . and the majority of the peasant population" be maintained.[30] Less than a month later he was noting: "Ten-twenty years of correct relations with the peasantry and victory is assured on a world scale (even with a delay in the proletarian revolutions, which are growing)." [31] Two years later, in his last articles, Lenin was even more preoccupied with the problem. "What if the complete hopelessness of the situation [of Russia in the world—M. J.], by intensifying tenfold the energies of the workers and peasants, offered us the possibility of proceeding to create the fundamental requirement of civilization in a way different from that of the West European countries?" he asked in January, 1923.

> . . . if a definite level of culture is required for the creation of socialism (although nobody can tell what that definite level of culture is), why cannot we begin by achieving the prerequisities for that definite level of culture in a revolutionary way, and *then*, with the help of a workers' and peasants' government and a Soviet system, proceed to overtake the other nations? . . . You say that civilization is necessary for the creation of socialism. Very good. But why could we not have begun by creating such prerequisites of civilization in our country as the expulsion of

---

[27] Quoted by Lenin, *Selected Works*, VII, p. 309.

[28] *Ibid.*, p. 297.

[29] *Selected Works*, IX, p. 227.

[30] *Ibid.*, p. 108.

[31] V. I. Lenin, *Polnoe Sobranie Sochineniy*, XLIII (Moscow, 1963), p. 383.

the landlords and the expulsion of the Russian capitalists, and
then start moving toward socialism? Where, in what books, have
you read that such variations of the customary historical order
of events are impermissible or impossible? [32]

Finally, in his article, "On Cooperation," Lenin wrote:

The power of the state over all large-scale means of production,
the power of the state in the hands of the proletariat, the alliance
of this proletariat with the many millions of small and very small
peasants, the assured leadership of the peasantry by the proletariat, etc.; is this not all that is necessary in order for the cooperatives . . . to build complete socialist society? This is not yet
the building of socialist society, but it is all that is necessary and
sufficient for this building. . . . A system of civilized cooperators
under the social ownership of the means of production, with the
class victory of the proletariat over the bourgeoisie, is socialism. [33]

Was Socialism Achieved?

The idea that Russia should aim to complete the building of
socialism on its own if the international revolution continued to be
delayed did represent a departure from the traditional theory of
the Bolsheviks, who had never foreseen their country finding itself
an isolated workers' state long enough for the question to arise.
But although it was never theoretically elaborated by Lenin, we
have seen how in the last period of his working life he was
coming more and more in practice to adopt such a perspective.
It was perfectly in keeping with Marxist theory that, after his
death, the party should come to terms with the new situation and
spell out its confidence that "NEP Russia will be transformed
into Socialist Russia" [Lenin] [34] by its own forces, if the revolution which all hoped for did not come in other countries and
alleviate their problems.

What did this perspective mean? Lenin had enumerated five
elements constituting the socioeconomic forms that existed in
Russia after the October Revolution, and into the period of the
New Economic Policy introduced in 1921: (1) patriarchal,

---

[32] *Selected Works*, VI, pp. 511–512. Lenin's italics.
[33] *Selected Works*, IX, pp. 403, 406.
[34] *Ibid.*, p. 381.

largely self-sufficient peasant economy; (2) small commodity production (including the majority of peasants selling their grain); (3) private capitalism; (4) state capitalism; and (5) socialism.[35] The transition to socialism was seen as meaning the transformation of Russia from a backward peasant land into a country with a modern centrally planned state industry and collective and state agriculture, accompanied by big educational and cultural advances. It meant the effective elimination of the first four of Lenin's socioeconomic categories, entailing the disappearance of the kulaks (rural bourgeoisie) and the Nep-men (merchant capitalists), and a vast growth of the fifth, comprising state-owned industry and state farms on the one hand, and collective farms on the other.[36] Defined in these terms, Stalin was able to say correctly after 1935 that Trotsky had been wrong, and that "our bourgeoisie has already been liquidated and socialism has already been built in the main. This is what we call the victory of socialism or, to be more exact, the victory of socialist construction in one country." [37]

To leave the problem there would, however, be all too facile. Not only had the collectivization of agriculture been carried out

[35] *Selected Works,* VII, p. 361. By state capitalism, Lenin meant here the control by the workers' state of capitalist producers and traders, who were permitted to operate "within certain limits." He distinguished it sharply from "the State capitalism which exists under the capitalist system when the State takes direct control of certain capitalist enterprises." (See IX, pp. 165–174, 338–339.) There is nothing in common between Lenin's concept of state capitalism as a progressive transitional form paving the way for Russia's advance to socialism in this early period, and the conceptions of state capitalism that have been advanced to give a basic characterization of the U.S.S.R. by, *inter alia,* Karl Kautsky, the Socialist Party of Great Britain, the International Socialism group, and the Maoists.

[36] In his article, *"On Cooperation,"* in *Selected Works,* IX, Lenin characterized this type of cooperative property, based on nationalization of the land, as socialist.

[37] Joseph Stalin, *The Final Victory of Socialism in the Soviet Union,* "Reply to Ivanov," February 2, 1938 (London, n.d.), pp. 3, 6. In his letter Stalin reiterated his long-standing position that "the final victory of Socialism, in the sense of full guarantee against the restoration of bourgeois property relations, is possible only on an international scale" and not so long as the Soviet Union was surrounded by numerous capitalist countries. (Pp. 6–7.)

in an unnecessarily costly and harsh manner that left profound distrust between important sections of the peasantry and the Soviet state, but political power and initiative were taken out of the hands of the working people and concentrated effectively in those of Stalin and a small irresponsible ruling group paternalistically substituting itself for them.[38] Stalin, in an extraordinarily difficult international situation, led the development and defense of the economic and cultural foundations of socialism—his great historical merit. But at the same time he rode roughshod over the democratic rights and organs of the party and the people, committing widespread arbitrary and brutal persecutions in which many of the finest Russian and foreign revolutionaries met a tragic end—his great crime, for which the Soviet Union and the international communist movement are still paying dearly today.

Since socialism and democracy have always been considered by Marxists to go hand in hand, Trotsky was on much stronger ground when, shifting his main line of argument, he came, in the second half of the thirties, to make lack of democracy his central objection to the claim that socialism had been built in Russia. He then indicated the police terror, the trumped-up Moscow Trials of Old Bolsheviks, and the general suppression of political freedom, preceded and accompanied by a great increase in the power of the degenerated bureaucratic apparatus in both the party and the state. What he failed to understand was that, for a certain period (which may be quite prolonged), an uneasy and antagonistic coexistence of a socialist economy and an undemocratic, unsocialist superstructure is possible. Sooner or later the development of the former will tend to push society (albeit tortuously, unevenly, and not at all "automatically") toward the reforming of the superstructure and its progressive alignment with the economic base—and with the desires of its progressively more developed and educated working class and intelligentsia.

This can only take place by means of sharp political struggles. Moreover on the economic plan what had been achieved

---

[38] I cannot go all the way with Krassó in his total rejection of the concept of "substitutionism" (*New Left Review*, 44, p. 66), which appears to me too sweeping. If an individual, group, or party act in the name of the working class while depriving it of its democratic right to decide the broad outlines of policy, this is substitution.

in the thirties was, of course, only the elements of socialism, which still needed many more decades of peaceful growth before it could fully overcome the terrible legacy of Russian backwardness and appear as a *fully developed* prosperous, harmonious, and cultured socialist society. The Soviet Union today, though immensely more advanced than in the thirties, has still a long way to go before completing this stage of socialist development. Talk of a transition to communism in the foreseeable future made in the Stalin and Khrushchev eras is now generally seen to have contained an enormous amount of bombast and extravagant claims. It is fair to say that Trotsky's writings do provide a useful corrective to this sort of hyperbole, which was described by Palmiro Togliatti as

> a prevailing tendency to exaggerate in the exaltation of achievements above all in the propaganda of that time, but also in the general presentation, and to consider all problems solved, and objective contradictions overcome—together with the difficulties and conflicts that are always inherent in the building of socialist society, and are liable to be very serious and insurmountable unless they are acknowledged openly.[39]

In criticizing the manifestations of national superiority, conceit, and narrow-mindedness, which went along with this and are unfortunately still far from extinct, Trotsky appealed correctly to the fundamentally internationalist traditions of Marxism, while wrongly arguing that what he was attacking flowed inevitably from the theory of socialism in one country.

The Revolution Betrayed

The Revolution Betrayed, written by Trotsky in 1936, shows both the strengths and weaknesses of his position at this time. Analyzing the development of the Soviet Union up to the mid-thirties, he scored quite a few bull's-eyes in exposing the negative effects of Stalinism on so many aspects of Russian life. However, many of his criticisms were carping and ill-conceived, such as his

---

[39] Palmiro Togliatti, *Questions Posed by the 20th Congress of the C.P.S.U.*, Interview with *Nuovi Argomenti* (London, 1956), p. 8.

attack on the terms of the 1936 Constitution, the weakness of which lay not in its extremely democratic provisions, but in their irrelevance to the real situation in the Soviet Union at that time, when Stalin could and did trample them underfoot. For instance, he described the introduction of the universal, equal, and direct vote, replacing the indirect system—the weighting of representation in favor of the working class as against the peasantry, and the denial of the vote to members of former exploiting classes—as "juridically liquidating the dictatorship of the proletariat." [40] The Constitution as a whole, he actually asserted, represented "an immense step back from socialist to bourgeois principles" and created "the political premises for the birth of a new possessing class." [41]

Trotsky's dogmatic shibboleth of the impossibility of building socialism in one country led him even now to underestimate how deeply entrenched and resilient the socialist system was in Russia, despite the ravages wrought by Stalin's purges. Without the interference of a revolution in the West, he claimed, if war should erupt, "the social bases of the Soviet Union must be crushed, not only in the case of defeat, but also in the case of victory." [42]

He went on to write that "the Soviet bureaucracy has gone far toward preparing a bourgeois restoration" and "must inevitably in future stages seek supports for itself in property relations" entailing "its conversion into a new possessing class." [43] In fact, of course, the victory of the Soviet in the war (Trotsky had pre-

---

[40] *The Revolution Betrayed*, p. 261.

[41] *Ibid.*, p. 272.

[42] *Ibid.*, p. 229. It is interesting to note that after the last war the Trotskyist Fourth International, far from making any self-criticism or analysis of this error, extolled its own "correctness" and proceeded to repeat the blunder. In its 1946 Manifesto, under the heading, "The Power of Marxist Prognosis," its International Conference claimed that "in every important respect the analysis of the Fourth International has stood the test of time" (*Workers International News* [London], April–May, 1946, p. 171), and went on in a resolution to state that "only the intervention of the proletarian revolution can prevent a fatal outcome for the U.S.S.R. in its present trial of strength with imperialism." (*Quatrième Internationale* [Paris], April–May, 1946, p. 18).

[43] L. Trotsky, *The Revolution Betrayed*, pp. 253–254.

dicted defeat [44]) was not followed by the slightest sign of a move toward a "bourgeois counterrevolution" [45] but, on the contrary, by the establishment—under the leadership of allegedly "counter-revolutionary" communist parties—of socialist property relations in thirteen other countries, and to the emergence of a world socialist system competing with the capitalist one. Moreover, since Stalin's death in 1953, the most negative features of Stalinism spotlighted by Trotsky have been dismantled. This "de-Staliniza-tion" has not occurred through the "inevitable" violent political revolution to overthrow the bureaucracy led by the Fourth International, as forecast and advocated in *The Revolution Betrayed*,[46] but essentially through the initiative of forces within the Communist Party(which Trotsky had written off as disintegrated,[47] "dead," [48] and "no longer the vanguard of the proletariat" [49]) and within "the bureaucracy," which, in Trot-sky's definition,[50] included all party, state, and collective farm leaders, managers, technicians, and foremen, drawn from among the most advanced sections of the working class and peasantry.

A fundamental Marxist critique of Stalinism still remains to be made. But it will not proceed from Trotsky's premises, although his writings should be studied for the many valuable lessons—both positive and negative—that they hold for us. Yet even where his insights are at their most brilliant, they occur within the framework of a fundamentally false sociological model that prevented him from understanding the laws of devel-opment of Soviet society or grasping the (admittedly new and un-precedented) phenomenon of Stalinism in its complexity and many-sidedness. Hence the unkindness with which history has treated the major predictions we have quoted in this article.

The source of most of Trotsky's errors in relation to Russia was already present in the years before World War I. "He some-

[44] *Ibid.*, p. 227.
[45] *Ibid.*, p. 290.
[46] *Ibid.*, pp. 284–290.
[47] L. Trotsky, *Stalinism and Bolshevism*, p. 8.
[48] *Ibid.*, p. 13.
[49] L. Trotsky, *The Revolution Betrayed*, p. 138.
[50] *Ibid.*, pp. 135. ff.

times seemed to view Russia's past and present almost as a vacuum," noted Deutscher.

> This was the weakness underlying his call for Europeanization and also the flaw in his attitude to Bolshevism. It was Lenin's strength that he took Russian reality as it was, while he set out to change it. Lenin's party had deep roots in Russian soil, and it absorbed all that that soil could yield in revolutionary strength and harshness, in world-shaking courage and in primitive crudity.[51]

Trotsky did not join that party until the eve of the October Revolution and never absorbed that tradition, remaining to a large extent a Western-oriented revolutionary intellectual. His pessimism toward the prospects of a socialist Russia was complemented by his much-vaunted "revolutionary optimism" toward prospects of revolution in the West and a strange belief that "optimism regarding an isolated proletarian state would entail pessimism toward the international revolution." [52] As Anatoly Lunacharsky showed in his sympathetic profile, Trotsky's "path to revolution . . . followed a straight line." [53] When history disproved his prognoses or ushered in new and unforeseen situations, he lacked Lenin's "sense of reality, which leads one now and then to alter one's tactics," and the "tremendous sensitivity to the demands of the time" that prompted Lenin "at one moment to sharpen both edges of his sword, at another to place it in its sheath." [54]

---

[51] Isaac Deutscher, *The Prophet Armed:* Trotsky 1879–1921 (London: Oxford University Press, 1954), p. 191.

[52] L. Trotsky, Letter on 15th Anniversary of October Revolution, October 13, 1932, in duplicated bulletin of Balham (Trotskyist) group, London, 1932.

[53] Anatoly Lunacharsky, *Revolutionary Silhouettes* (London, 1967), p. 67.

[54] *Loc. cit.*

MONTY JOHNSTONE

Reply to Ernest Mandel

In his reply to my article, Ernest Mandel continues to distort the real issues involved in the debate on "socialism in one country," as well as misrepresenting my argument. I see this as a regrettable case of blurred vision arising from an apparently deeply felt "need" to notice only what contributes to the "vindication" of Trotsky.

This is doubtless why he writes that I tried "to convince my readers that the debate of 1926 was centered around the possibility or impossibility of developing the productive forces and industrializing the U.S.S.R., whereas it was precisely Trotsky (alleged 'skeptical about the internal forces of Russian socialism') who was the great advocate of accelerated industrialization." In fact, on the very first page of my article, I wrote: "Trotsky never disputed the need to start the job of building socialism, and advanced proposals for an increased rate of economic growth to this end." (*New Left Review,* 50, pp. 113–114.) I then went on to point to the unresolved contradiction between these ambitious proposals and Trotsky's arguments over the years that no "genuine rise of socialist economy in Russia" was possible until the victory of revolution in the West, without which the country would allegedly return to capitalism. This perspective excluded not only the possibility of Russia by its internal forces achieving

145

socialism, in *whichever* way one defines it, but ruled out even its survival as a workers' state. It has been refuted by history. On this crucial point Mandel prefers to remain silent.

As I pointed out, the controversy was waged in somewhat elusive terms. Hence the conceptions of socialism held by its participants were neither uniform nor clear-cut. Moreover it is perfectly possible to produce a whole variety of definitions of socialism used at different times and in different contexts by Lenin (or by Trotsky, Stalin, or other Russian revolutionary leaders) that appear to contradict each other. What is important is the kernel of the conception common to them all—"the generally accepted sense of their word," as Lenin called it in *State and Revolution* [1]—namely, collective, as opposed to private, ownership of the means of production. Trotsky's definition of 1906—"cooperative production on a large scale"—accords as fully with this traditional view as does Lenin's similar view of 1923 that I also quoted: "A system of civilized cooperators under the social ownership of the means of production, with the class victory of the proletariat over the bourgeoisie, is socialism."

Mandel alleges that this "preposterous" definition of what was meant by building socialism in one country was an *ex post facto* invention of Stalin's, which he did not "dare" to introduce until 1936! One is confronted with a veritable *embarras du choix* in deciding what to quote in refutation to this breathtaking assertion. Thus, when Stalin in April, 1924, spoke, at the time negatively, of the possibility of the victory of socialism in one country, he presented this as synonymous with "the organization of socialist *production.*" [2] Trotsky was to express his approval of this formulation.[3] In January, 1925, Stalin, who was now arguing the feasibility of socialism in one country, explained that "the point at issue" was "the victory of socialism in general, i.e., driving away the landlords and capitalists, taking power, repelling the attacks of imperialism and beginning to build a socialist economy." [4]

---

[1] V. I. Lenin, *Collected Works,* XXI/2 (New York, n.d.), p. 223.

[2] Joseph Stalin, *The Theory and Practice of Leninism* (London, 1925), p. 45. My italics.

[3] Leon Trotsky, *The Third International After Lenin* (New York, 1957), p. 36.

[4] J. Stalin, *Works,* VII (Moscow, 1954), p. 16.

It was, moreover, not just a question of how individual leaders understood the question, but of the conception of the great majority of the party. Later that year, the Fourteenth Party Congress, the first at which this question was debated (though Trotsky chose to remain silent throughout and not to join in the controversy until 1926), viewed the question in precisely the way that I indicated in my article. Its main resolution declared:

> In the field of *economic construction* the party congress proceeds from the fact that our country, the country of the dictatorship of the proletariat, possesses "all that is necessary in order to build complete socialist society" [Lenin] . . . Inside the economy, alongside all the diversity of its component parts (peasant natural economy, small commodity production, private capitalism, state capitalism and socialism) the share of *socialist* industry, of state and cooperative trade, of nationalized credit and of other commanding heights of the proletarian state is markedly increasing. In this way an *economic offensive* of the proletariat and an advance of the economy of the U.S.S.R. directed toward socialism is under way.[5]

Lastly, in Stalin's report to the Fifteenth Party Congress, shortly before the passage quoted by Mandel, Stalin said: "The possibility of the victory of socialism in our country means nothing more nor less than the possibility of the victory of the socialist elements over the capitalist elements" through the internal forces of the Russian Revolution.[6] As the record shows—and it is to be hoped that the reader will examine it for himself with an open mind—it was precisely such a victory of which Trotsky again and again disputed the possibility, as I claim amply to have demonstrated in my article.

In his concern to justify his claim that Russian Communists saw socialism as incompatible with the existence of commodities, money, and the state, Mandel makes a particularly clumsy attempt to dismiss Lenin's classical definition in *State and Revolution* (in *Collected Works* [New York, n.d.]) of the distinctions between socialism and communism. Even Grigory Zinoviev, ar-

---

[5] *Die kommunistische Partei der Sowjetunion in Resolutionen und Beschlussen der Parteitage, Konferenzen und Plenen des Z. K.,* VI (Berlin, 1957), pp. 6–7. Italics in original.

[6] J. Stalin, *op. cit.,* VIII, pp. 274, 277.

guing in 1925 against the theory of socialism in one country, described the formulations given in the passages that I so "impudently" quoted as "the most precise given by Leninism." [7] Lenin's statement that "for the complete withering away of the state complete communism is necessary" shows very clearly that he saw a stateless society as belonging only to what Marx called the higher stage of communism—*not,* as Mandel argues, to its lower, socialist, one. This was recognized even by Trotsky, in 1936, when he wrote in *The Revolution Betrayed:* "In a communist society, the state and money will disappear. Their gradual dying away ought consequently to *begin* under socialism." [8] Mandel merely mixes up the beginning with the end of the process! Certainly, however, in terms of its internal functions (as opposed to its external defense role) it is a grave weakness that the Soviet state has moved in the opposite direction with grossly inflated powers being enforced by a bureaucratic apparatus not subject to effective popular control.

The 1919 Party Program was quite emphatic that "prior to the organization of a *fully developed* system of *communist* production and distribution of goods, the abolition of money is impossible." [9] Leaving aside some utopian ideas from the period of War Communism, what was envisaged and has in fact taken place has been a reduction in the spheres of operation of money. Thus, in 1930, it ceased to be used in transactions between state enterprises and organizations except as an accounting unit used for bookkeeping entries at the nationalized banks.[10] Likewise the field of action of commodity production, which the existence of money presupposes but from which the capital goods sector has in general been removed, has been strictly regulated and restricted by the socialist state, which dominates the whole economy. When Lenin spoke of commodity production constantly reproducing the danger of primitive accumulation of capital, he was thinking of the millions of private peasants and independent producers

---

[7] *Staline contre Trotsky* (Paris, 1965), p. 192.

[8] L. Trotsky, *The Revolution Betrayed* (New York, 1957), p. 65. My italics.

[9] Nikolai Bukharin and Evgeny Preobrazhensky, *The ABC of Communism* (London, 1924), p. 408. My italics.

[10] See, e.g., C. Bettelheim, *La Planification Sovietique* (Paris, 1945), p. 56.

and traders of the early years after the revolution. The disappearance of such groups completely changed the position, as Mandel knows full well. It removed the last possible basis for the revival of private capitalism within Russia that Trotsky so frequently and so erroneously predicted, and it is quite incredible to find Mandel raising that bogey again today.

The Soviet Union by the mid-thirties realized the core of Lenin's conception of a classless society: all incomes derived from the ownership of land and capital, all exploitation of one class by another, had been eliminated. Although, it is true, not a society without any classes, there was no necessary basis for class *antagonisms* between the two that remained: the workers and the collective-farm peasants working in socialist enterprises of different types and levels within the framework of a national plan based on national ownership of industry and the land.[11]

This is not to say, by any means, that a fully developed harmonious socialist society in transition to communism has been built, as official Soviet propaganda has claimed. Not only are the levels of the consumer goods industries, housing, and transport, not to speak of agriculture, too low to be able to speak in such terms for a long time to come; it is also a question of the undemocratic, unsocialist political superstructure, of which I spoke in my first article and which, above all, tragically disfigures Soviet society. Here, after the spasmodic and uneven leaps forward between 1953 and 1962, the initiative has passed for the time being to "hard-line" elements conducting a vigorous counteroffensive from positions of power in the party and state. Although there has not by any means been a full-scale return to the position in Stalin's time, we have been witnessing an alarming strengthening of Stalinist forces, tendencies, and practices (highlighted by political and cultural repression and by the invasion of Czechoslovakia), against which in its turn an embryonic anti-Stalinist communist opposition is taking shape. To characterize the eco-

---

[11] That is not to say that there are not class differences, even substantial ones, between them, nor that their interests cannot diverge. Such divergences, whether real or apparent, should, however, be seen as being in many respects akin to sectional divisions of interest within, say, the working class, rather than as constituting class "interests which are antagonistic historically," as Mandel alleges in his *Marxist Economic Theory*, Vol. 2 (London, 1968), p. 565.

nomic foundations of the Soviet Union since the mid-thirties as socialist no more implies approval of its bureaucratic and repressive features than did Trotsky's insistence, while to his great credit he exposed Stalin's far more terrible purges, that Russia was despite all a "workers' state."

Notwithstanding the terribly low level at which it had to start and the drastic limitations of democracy, the U.S.S.R. has been able to show the world the advantages of what Lenin called socialist production,[12] with an outstanding rate of industrial development sustained over several decades. The further development of this socialist economic base cannot in the long run fail to have a decisive effect on the political superstructure of the country, although undoubtedly in a more drawn-out, complicated, and at times stormy manner than many of us foresaw in the aftermath of the Twentieth Congress. To lump together the Russia of 1936, or *a fortiori* of today, with the qualitatively different Russia of 1919 with its undeveloped mixed economy, categorizing them both as transitional regimes between capitalism and socialism, seems to me curious, confusing, and un-Marxist. It provides the wrong framework for understanding the main trends of Soviet development, as I believe a critical examination of Trotsky's prognoses shows all too clearly.

[12] In contrast, Mandel, when writing of the Soviet economy, prefers to speak of "the contradictory combination of a *noncapitalist* mode of production and a still basically bourgeois mode of distribution." (*Ibid.*, pp. 565, 572. My italics.) Even so, in describing this combination, he is unwittingly reproducing the essence of Lenin's famous definition of socialist (as opposed to communist) society in *State and Revolution:* the abolition of bourgeois right by the proletarian state in respect of the means of production, alongside its retention (and "protection" by the state) in the sphere of distribution. (Lenin, *op. cit.*, p. 224.) Far from having modified this understanding of socialism by the time that he wrote *Economics and Politics in the Era of the Dictatorship of the Proletariat* in October, 1919, as Mandel alleges, we find him in December, 1919, making the same distinction between socialism and communism as in 1917. "Socialism," he reiterated then, "is the society that grows directly out of capitalism, that is the first form of the new society." It implied "the performance of work without the aid of capitalists" but with the "strictest accounting, control and supervision" and fixing the "standards for labor and the amount of compensation for labor." The economic system existing in Russia at that time was "a process in which the foundations of socialism (were) being laid in large-scale production." (Lenin, *Selected Works,* VIII, pp. 239, 241.)

C. J. ARTHUR

The Coming Soviet Revolution

In spite of Trotsky's tremendous role in the victory of the Russian Revolution, his name will forever be associated primarily with the struggle against its decline, with his patient exposures of Stalin's falsifications of the program and history of the revolution. The unprecedented and unforeseen problems associated with the decline of the revolution confronted Marxism with an acute crisis of theory and practice. No one should deny Trotsky the foremost place among those who seriously faced up to them on the basis of uncompromising revolutionary principle.

Unfortunately Nicolas Krassó's critique of "Trotsky's Marxism" almost ignores his analysis of Stalin's Russia. Trotsky's main work in this field, *The Revolution Betrayed,* (1936) still has not been superseded. Krassó can find no objection to the work other than its "demagogic title." Indeed, Krassó seems to accept much of Trotsky's position on this question: "When many of his followers were manufacturing new 'ruling classes' and 'capitalist restorations' in the Soviet Union at will, Trotsky, in his analysis of the Soviet state and party apparatus emphasized, on the contrary, that it was not a social class." [1] One might add that the steadiness of Trotsky's vision also contrasts favorably with the outpourings of those who now invent "new Tsars" at will.

It would, however, be surprising in the extreme if this first attempt, even by a very capable Marxist, to grasp theoretically

---

[1] Nicolas Krassó, *New Left Review*, 44, p. 85.

the meaning of the horrors of Stalinism had succeeded, given the unforeseen nature of the circumstances. I think one can detect a certain forcing of the Marxist categories in Trotsky's attempt to comprehend the new material and to adapt the revolutionary program to the new tasks. Here I try to argue in a tentative way that the concepts relied on in *The Revolution Betrayed* do not adequately grasp the dialectic of transition from capitalism to socialism. In doing so I believe I am dealing with a major portion of Trotsky's contribution to Marxism, which has so far not been adequately assessed.

The received doctrine, shared by all groups basing themselves on the Fourth International (which Trotsky founded in 1938), revolves around the trinity of concepts: (a) workers' state; (b) political revolution; and, opposing the latter (c) social revolution. The doctrine holds that a bureaucratic degeneration or deformation has occurred and requires a political revolution to establish socialism proper, but that no social revolution is required because capitalist property relations have already, broadly speaking, been replaced. The objection that a workers' state can hardly be said to exist when the workers have no rights and are tyrannized by bureaucratic gangsters is circumvented by pointing out that the political form of bourgeois dictatorships can vary from parliamentary to fascist without affecting the social base of society because the latter is determined primarily by the economic form. Even the Bonapartes, who could not give a damn for the susceptibilities of the so-called ruling class, and who dip their fingers in the till as they please, have to have the till filled up somehow; and how this is done determines the nature of society.

It is this doctrine—and in particular the idea that we can so slickly counterpose political and social revolution in our program —that I propose to reexamine.

Preliminaries

In the first place, let us note the unfortunate ambiguity in the term "workers' state." By this, of course, we mean the basic character of society as a whole. The state in the narrower sense of the word (i.e., the institutions of coercion) is acknowledged by Trotsky not to be in the hands of the proletariat, but in those of the party bureaucracy that has expropriated the proletariat politically. Even so, it is held that insofar as the interests of the bureaucracy itself are connected with nationalized property, it will in some way be likely to defend the latter against capitalist encroachment and thus be, in part, a defender of proletarian interests.

So far, so good. However, the neat political-social dichotomy begins to disintegrate when Trotsky argues that it is inexplicable how such a degeneration could occur solely at the political level, and he rounds out his account of the political expropriation of the proletariat by giving this a *social basis:*

> This whole stratum, which does not engage directly in productive labor, but administers, orders, commands, pardons, and punishes—leaving aside teachers and students—must be numbered at five or six million. . . .
>
> In the whole mass of the bureaucracy, the communists together with the Communist Youth constitute a block of one and a half to two million—at present, owing to continued purgations, rather less than more. This is the backbone of the state power. These communist administrators are the backbone of the party, and of the Communist Youth. The former Bolshevik party is now no longer the vanguard of the proletariat, but the political organization of the bureaucracy. . . . Hypothetically, we may assume that the labor and collectivized peasant aristocracy, the Stakhanovists, the nonparty "actives," trusted personages, their relatives and relatives-in-law, approximate the same figure that we adopted for the bureaucracy, that is, five to six million. . . . Twelve percent, or perhaps fifteen percent of the population—that is the authentic social basis of the autocratic ruling circles.[2]

Thus Trotskyists always argue that even the personal dictatorship of Stalin had social roots in a stratum of society, and that Trotsky had little difficulty in showing that this stratum had very considerable material privileges that sharply differentiated its interests from those of the masses.

A question that immediately arises is: if, even allowing for the relative autonomy of the political sphere, we find that this political expropriation has a *social basis* in such a stratum, can we talk about a merely political revolution when such a revolution

---

[2] Leon Trotsky, *The Revolution Betrayed* (New York, 1965 edition), pp. 138–139.

would clearly involve dispossessing this stratum not only of its political expression, but also of its material privileges? Especially when Trotsky estimates that over twelve percent of the population may be involved?

In *The Revolution Betrayed* Trotsky bases his analysis, in the main, on antagonisms in the sphere of distribution stemming from a low level of productivity. However, far more important than its effect on distribution will be the effect of the so-called political revolution on production itself. Trotsky does not stress this, partially because of the "administrative" bent that Lenin undoubtedly noted, partially again perhaps because the low level of the masses in his day makes my point academic—namely the social character of production in the Soviet Union imposes fetters on the most important productive force of all, the initiative and creativity of the worker himself. The completely hierarchical command structure of the Soviet economy makes the individual worker the same kind of labor-power machine and nothing more than he is in a capitalist factory. Who can doubt that a new upsurge of proletarian revolution, sweeping away bureaucratic privilege, would also restructure production itself so as to provide avenues of expression for the enthusiasm and ingenuity of the workers? It is not at all a question of the CPSU right wing and the bourgeois press duet, of personnel changes (i.e., the replacement of politically reliable but stupid cadres with technically competent ones), but of the entry of an educated working class into the arena. Such an access of strength to the productive forces again requires us to ask if it can be comprehended by a mere political revolution.

Moreover (if with some trepidation), one is also forced to speak of cultural revolution here. A new upsurge of proletarian revolution in the Soviet Union could not possibly succeed in changing organizational forms in abstraction from the forms of thought, values, and character of the population. It is perfectly clear that, in many respects, bourgeois values and ideology, superstition, religion, and all kinds of vice profoundly permeate Soviet society.

One small example from Wolfgang Leonhard's *Child of the Revolution* illustrates this. He relates that in Berlin, in October, 1945, a communist from the West, who had spent the war underground, accosted him in the Central Committee building.

"I am a K.P.D. official invited here from the West. I have been given some chits for meals, but I don't know where the dining room is."

"That depends what sort of ticket you have."

He looked at me in surprise and showed me his ticket. It was Category III—a ticket for less important members of staff. I showed him the way.

"But tell me—are the meals different for different members of staff in the Central Committee?"

"Yes, of course. There are four different kinds of ticket, according to the class of work one is doing. The last two categories are for technicians and clerks."

"Yes, but . . . aren't they all members of the Party?"

"Yes, of course. They are all certified Party members, including the charwomen and chauffeurs and night watchmen."

He looked at me in astonishment and said, "Different tickets —different meals—and they are all members of the Party!"

He turned and went without another word. A moment later I heard the creak of the front door. My comrade had left the Central Committee building. Thoughtfully I crossed the courtyard to the dining room. I went through the rooms in which Categories III and IV—the lower classes—were fed: and for the first time I had an uneasy feeling as I opened the door into the dining room reserved for our category. Here, at a table covered with a white cloth, the senior members of staff enjoyed an excellent meal of several courses. "Curious," I thought, "that this has never struck me before!" [3]

What is important in this example is not so much that such a hierarchy exists but that no one thinks it particularly odd. Values have to change with the structures—large-scale transformations of people's understanding of themselves and their social relationships—if socialism is to come out of this.

The Basis of the Degeneration

There is another vulgar Trotskyist thesis that warrants attention before we proceed. It is held that the case of the Soviet Union and its degeneration is an "exception," easily explicable by certain special circumstances that we have no reason to expect generally:

---

[3] Wolfgang Leonhard, *Child of the Revolution* (London, 1957), p. 377.

backwardness, isolation, encirclement, and so on. However, though it is obvious enough that the circumstances cited clearly conditioned the development, the "exception" theory begins to appear oversimple when we consider other experiences. There are now some dozen or more "workers' states" and, although there are enormous differences between them, none of them corresponds to the expected "model" of socialism. (This leads some undialectical thinkers of an either-or type simply to reject them as capitalist, based on brutal logic [formal] and the capacity to fly in the face of realities.)

All these regimes, like the U.S.S.R., are in various ways in a transitional state somewhere between capitalism (or colonialism) and socialism. Indeed, only abstract moralizers with no Marxist understanding could fail to expect that a more or less long period of transition toward socialism is unavoidable. Furthermore, this period cannot be expected to be one of continuous, smooth transition; it, too, must have its dialectic, its periods of decline and renewal. It should be stressed that historical experience proves that *any* revolution inevitably undergoes a period of ebb, of degeneration, and that its severity depends on the circumstances. In a sense, therefore, the swift rise of bureaucratism in postrevolutionary Russia was conditioned not only by the allegedly exceptional circumstances of the time; it must also be understood as having, in addition, endemic roots in the revolutionary process itself.

When the Left Opposition was grappling with the frightening phenomena of degeneration, Khristian Rakovsky was the one who saw this most clearly. Trotsky justly quotes his document on the subject several times in *The Revolution Betrayed*.

In his analysis of the "professional dangers" of power Rakovsky stressed:

> I do not refer here to the objective difficulties due to the whole complex of historical conditions, to the capitalist encirclement on the outside, and to the pressure of the petite bourgeoisie inside the country. No, I refer to the inherent difficulties of any new directing class, consequent on the taking and on the exercise of power itself, on the ability or inability to make use of it.[4]

---

[4] Khristian Rakovsky, "The Professional Dangers of Power," in *The Bulletin of Marxist Studies*, No. 3 (1968), p. 19.

The main such inherent feature is that proletarians, upon taking power, do not automatically become supermen. They are the same proletarians whose behavior before the revolution fluctuated wildly—to the degree that their confidence rose and sank, limited by their political and cultural experience. The revolutionary seizure of power by a previously oppressed class that has lived all its life under the hegemony of another class is, by definition, an extraordinarily high peak of activity, unity, and consciousness on its part. Is it surprising that, when all problems are not solved the day after taking power, the revolutionary tide begins to ebb?

Apathy, cynicism, fragmentation, selfishness, and withdrawal disperse the masses from the stage of history again, leaving behind the apparatus cast out by them; but it is no longer representative of, or controlled by, the class in whose name it rules. Now the way is open for negative developments in the apparatus itself, developments that reinforce the demoralization of the class. There follow bureaucratic arrogation of power and privilege, careerism, and corruption, until finally, instead of expressing the dictatorship of the proletariat, the apparatus exercises dictatorship over the proletariat. How far such tendencies actually go, of course, will be determined by the kind of circumstances usually cited in explaining the degeneration that took place. Also, it goes without saying that, in this case, we do not have simply an objective process but one that is mediated by particular people and their subjectivity—Stalin, etc.—so that there is a certain openness about the situation, within which subjective factors (e.g., Stalin's jealousy and suspiciousness) help to determine the outcome. Nevertheless, as Marxists, we must recognize that the objective forces do set limits to what even the greatest individual can achieve.

It is not a question of saying that if Trotsky had been leader, he would have done the same as Stalin. That is horribly abstract. For Trotsky to have been at the head of affairs, either the objective circumstances would have had to be different from what they were, or Trotsky would have had to have been . . . Stalin!

From any objective consideration, the Left Opposition was doomed to defeat. That is not to say that their struggle was worthless, that they should have helped Stalin or retired into private life. Apart from the psychological impossibility of such a course by a man like Trotsky, they were not in a position at the time to know all the relevant considerations. It was always possible that some new revolutionary breakthrough in the West might have come to the aid of the U.S.S.R., which would have changed the conditions of their struggle. Then again it could be argued that a stubborn rearguard action might ameliorate or slow down a process of degeneration. Finally, it is possible for a revolutionary tendency, even if defeated, to make a positive contribution from the long-term point of view; for when a new upsurge of the revolution comes, it can go back and learn from the struggle and analyses of the heroic groups that kept alive the program of revolution instead of capitulating to "realities." That is why *The Revolution Betrayed* is still an important book today—because it represents not only the dying embers of one revolutionary upsurge but also a point of renewal for the future.

To return to the main point: we have enough experience of transitional regimes to see now that tendencies toward bureaucratic degeneration are *endemic* to the transitional situation, are internal to it, and would have to be guarded against even if imperialism did not exist.

All these preliminary questions impel us to attempt to develop a more sophisticated methodology for analyzing transitional regimes.

One must grasp the fact that the historical dialectic is not one-dimensional; neither are its phases of a single amplitude. Indeed, it might be more accurate to speak of an infinitely large number of dialectics; of differing social levels (economic, ideological, etc.); of differing historical specificity (contrary to Herbert Marcuse in *Reason and Revolution: Hegel and the Rise of Social Theory* [1960], there is no reason to suppose that with the abolition of classes dialectic becomes obsolete); and of differing generality with regard to space and time (thus, from the point of view of a very general historical dialectic, proletarian revolution may represent a *simple* moment of transition, but judged internally it reveals enormous complexities that require a more specific historical analysis to supplement the other). Those who think that all that dialectics has to say about the transition from capitalism to socialism is that *bourgeoisie versus proletariat* results in *classless society,* or the relations of *private property versus socialized productive forces* results in a *socialist mode of production* —or even both—inevitably fall into mechanist or fatalistic views with regard to questions posed at more concrete levels. They tend to reduce the related but autonomous dialectics to a single simple contradiction, and they treat transitional phases with the criteria of formal abstract categories (often of a highly "moral" content) instead of grasping their historicity, seeing them as moments of a development, and analyzing their specific contradictions.

What I am pointing to here, to put it crudely, is the "Chinese-box" character of the historical dialectic: we have totalities within totalities, dialectics within dialectics.

This involves not only seeing that the transitional period has its own phases and stages, but also seeing that an epoch like capitalism is not just a stage in history but has its own history, i.e., it is made up of a series of transitions. It does not just grow smoothly up to its limit; it has its own internal dialectic in which various subordinate contradictions work themselves out and fetters are overcome. The Common Market project, for example, is an outstanding case of an attempt by the more farsighted European capitalists to overcome the fetters of tariffs and piddling markets, and to resolve the contradictions between national capitals, by creating European firms in a European market.

Once one gets away from concentrating on the single simple, global contradiction and begins to develop the idea of the dialectics of different levels of specificity, it begins to seem less extraordinary that postrevolutionary societies may exhibit all kinds of contradictions and may ossify into various forms of partial supercession of previous conditions, and that these forms then become obstacles to further development.

The disjunction political revolution/social revolution obscures this reality because it locates the trouble (at any rate, in its terminology) at only one level, thus introducing a radical discrepancy between this level and others. In fact, a more sophisticated analysis would surely show contradictions at other levels. The terminology is an attempt to express theoretically the progressive character of Soviet society vis-à-vis capitalism; but because of poverty-stricken methodological assumptions it can only visualize being able to do this by locating its "good side" in the base and its "bad side" in the superstructure.

There is a utopian, apocalyptic strain in Marxism that views socialism as the final resolution of all contradictions. Personally, I take such talk with a grain of salt, preferring to regard such a resolution as an asymptotic limit never reached. In particular, I reject Marcuse's claim (in *Reason and Revolution*) that since the dialectic was developed to analyze the history of class societies, socialism makes it obsolete, and the new development must be understood as a "purely rational" one. I see no reason for reducing the manifold contradictions of social life to a single class-based dialectic. If one considers this purely rational social development, would it not presuppose that social structures were perfectly transparent, that individuals knew exactly what all other individuals were thinking and had instant means of mediating their activity? (There is also the relation of society to nature to consider.) This looks suspiciously like the reinsertion of Hegel's absolute.

Curiously enough, the Maoists characterize Liu Shao-ch'i in a similar way: "In the opinion of [Liu] communist society is a bed of roses, without darkness or contradiction; all is well, without the existence of opposites. . . . What [Liu] is doing here is preaching metaphysics." [5]

Surely we must recognize that although you can define the development of socialism as proceeding from the free decisions of voluntarily associated producers, this is easier said than done. In any complex society there is always the possibility that the institutions that mediate the activity of people can grow away from them, and become so independent and autonomous that eventually antagonisms begin to make themselves felt, requiring a new adjustment in order to restore harmony. (See Lenin on the trade union controversy.)

Alienation

The language of the last sentence has an obvious bearing on the question of alienation. Does alienation exist in "workers' states"—and if so, what?

Once again one should guard against reductionism and for-

---

[5] *Peking Review*, May 12, 1967, p. 9.

malism. On the one hand, at the Kafka Conference organized by the Czechs some years ago, the East German delegates stoutly maintained that there was no alienation in their country because alienation is obviously a characteristic of capitalism. On the other hand, the ultraleft C. L. R. James agrees with the equivalence, but concludes that because alienation obviously exists in these societies they must be capitalist! [6] These complementary views clearly rest on the crude assumption that, with the expropriation of the capitalists, all problems, including that of alienation, are resolved.

It is necessary to stress that the category of alienation is an extremely general one that permeates capitalist society in many ways, expressing itself in different manifestations. Very generally, one can define a process, or state, of alienation as one in which certain expressions of human powers, or activity, become lost to their originator, assume an independent form, and become external, hostile determinants of his behavior.

The concept has been used in the critique of religion (e.g., in Ludwig Feuerbach), of the state (in Marx's early critique of Hegel), of capital (in *Economic and Philosophical Manuscripts of 1844* and *Capital*), of commodities (again in *Capital,* especially the section on commodity fetishism), and of capitalist consumption (e.g., in Fromm).

It is clear from the generality of the definition that, although alienation, reification, fetishism, and the rest are especially acute in capitalist society, one can apply the category to features of a different historical specificity by discerning the particular ways, the specific structures, that can helpfully be described in these terms without assuming that we are thereby dealing with a single system.

The form of alienation that is historically specific to capitalism is that which expresses itself in the rule of private property or, more concretely, of capital and of commodities, which are, of course, products of alienated labor. The relations between men in production are mediated by one form of estrangement, namely, capital. The relation between producers and consumers is mediated by a related form of estrangement—the fetishism of commodities. These mediations constitute the profoundly antihuman content of capitalist society. That is, if one asks, when two men go into a factory, why one can boss the other, the answer cannot be

---

[6] See *International Socialism,* No. 16.

given in terms of any human characteristics, such as superior intelligence, force of personality, or something else. The answer has to be given in terms of their differing relation to the nonhuman entity—capital. That is why Marx so often talks not about the rule of the capitalists, but of the "rule of dead matter." Capital mediates, and even seems to determine, the relation of one man to another. Of course, in this relationship the capitalist finds confirmation of his power, whereas the worker is subjected. Even more ironic is the fact that capital itself is nothing but crystallized labor, so that the worker is being subjected to the externalized product of his own activity. The more he works, the more products he produces for the capitalists, the more surplus value is realized by the sale of these products, and the greater grows the store of capital possessed by the capitalist, the non-possession of which determines the worker's subordination. So we see that in his activity the worker continually reproduces the means of his own domination!

"Dead matter" also rules in the sphere of commodity exchange. Relations between producers and consumers are mediated by, and disguised as, relations between things. The latter relations, the exchange values, Marx says, are determined "behind the backs" of the producers and, in association with the general compulsion to accumulate capital, condition what is produced.

Now, what happens when all the important concentrations of capital, and external trade, are expropriated by the revolution and constituted state property? Clearly this must have a drastic impact on the laws of motion of the economy; it must profoundly modify the character of the estrangements constitutive of previous times, and represent the first step in the supercession of specifically capitalist forms of estrangement. It can hardly be said that the accumulation of capital and the movement of the commodity market determine production in the U.S.S.R. in the same crucial way that they do under capitalism, although they clearly still play a greater or lesser role (in the case of Yugoslavia, greater). For example, the power of man over man is now no longer mediated by capital—rather, we have an *administrative* hierarchy (such as you might have in the army or civil service).

It is true, of course, that state property still plays a mediating role and that this constitutes a form of estrangement. However (as a matter of fact, just as private property), this moment is a historical necessity. In this connection, Trotsky points out:

> In order to become social, private property must as inevitably pass through the state stage as the caterpillar in order to become a butterfly must pass through the pupal stage. But the pupa is not a butterfly. . . . State property becomes the property of "the whole people" only to the degree that social privilege and differentiation disappear, and therewith the necessity of the state.[7]

Clearly, though, in the case of the U.S.S.R., state property is more than a convenient juridical mediation because of the role played by the bureaucracy, which Trotsky did not hesitate to compare with the fascist bureaucracy.

There has always been a somewhat intractable problem of locating the state bureaucracy in the class structure of society. Marx criticized very early Hegel's idealization of bureaucracy; in a striking passage in *The 18th Brumaire* he writes:

> This executive power, with its enormous bureaucratic and military organization, with its ingenious state machinery, embracing wide strata, with a host of officials numbering a half-million, besides an army of another half-million, this appalling parasitic body which enmeshes the body of French society like a net and chokes all its pores. . . .

This is very reminiscent of Trotsky's description of the Soviet bureaucracy. However, the problem is compounded here by two further features:

> In no other regime has a bureaucracy ever achieved such a degree of independence from the dominating class. In bourgeois society, the bureaucracy represents the interests of a possessing and educated class, which has at its disposal innumerable means of everyday control over its administration of affairs. The Soviet bureaucracy has risen above a class which is hardly emerging from destitution and darkness, and has no tradition of dominion or command. . . .
>
> . . . the very fact of its appropriation of political power in a country where the principal means of production are in the hands of the state creates a new and hitherto unknown relation

---

[7] L. Trotsky, *The Revolution Betrayed*, p. 237.

between the bureaucracy and the riches of the nation. The means of production belong to the state. But the state, so to speak, "belongs" to the bureaucracy.[8]

We shall have to return to this "hitherto unknown relation," but here I want to argue that, from the point of view of the analysis of the degree of estrangement involved, one must still insist that the character of the subordination of the proletariat by the bureaucracy is distinct from that of its subordination to capital. One way of seeing this is to approach it through Marx's analyses of commodity fetishism in *Capital*. In commodity production "it is a definite social relation between men that assumes, in their eyes, the fantastic form of a relation between things." He then goes on to contrast this with *feudal production:*

> . . . for the very reason that personal dependence forms the groundwork of society, there is no necessity for labor and its products to assume a fantastic form different from their reality. They take the shape, in the transactions of society, of services in kind and payments in kind . . . every serf knows that what he expends in the service of his lord is a definite quantity of his own personal labor power. . . . The social relations between individuals in the performance of their labor appear at all events as their own mutual personal relations, and are not disguised under the shape of social relations between the products of labor.

Again Marx contrasts commodity relations with a community carrying on its work with the means of production held in common, in which the labor power of individuals is consciously applied as the combined power of the community. Here the total product is a social product. Labor time would be apportioned in accordance with a definite social plan tailored to the real needs of the community.

"The social relations of the individual producers, with regard both to their labor and to its products, are in this case perfectly simple and intelligible. . . ."

It seems that one can plausibly argue that the structures and associated consciousness of Soviet society can to a great extent be contrasted with capitalist society in a similar way. Social relations would seem to appear as mutual personal relations rather

---

[8] *Ibid.,* pp. 248–249.

than take the fantastic form of things. Every worker knows who it is that is pushing him around—from the factory manager up to the Presidium. It is partly because the bureaucracy cannot cloak its privileges with the mystifications of commodity fetishism that a huge apparatus of physical repression is needed. The irrationalities of the Soviet economy are not so hidden as those in capitalism. If a sudden shortage or surplus of some product occurs, everyone knows that "the bureaucrats have messed it up again." There is some individual, identifiable in principle, who was too busy lining his own pockets or ensuring his political survival to perform his role in the planning system efficiently. In spite of the existence of the mediation of state property, the relationships of subordination seem defined primarily in terms of personal dependence—though, of course, unlike the identity of person and social position under feudalism, the bureaucrat in his person is only contingently related to his official position. It is an administrative hierarchy open to talent (of a sort!).

However, although state property represents the negation of private property, this antithesis is still posed within the sphere of property, i.e., of estrangement. As Marx observes, in connection with what he calls "crude communism":

"The category of laborer is not done away with, but extended to all men. The relationship of private property persists in the relationship of the community to the world of things." [9]

Again:

> The community is only a community of labor, and of equality of *wages* paid out by the communal capital—the *community* as the universal capitalist. Both sides of the relationship are raised to an imagined universality—*labor* as a state in which every person is put, and *capital* as the acknowledged universality and power of the community.[10]

State property is therefore, par excellence, an intermediate form. From one point of view it is the first form of communism; from another, the final term of the property system, universalized private property—hence property in the process of being negated.

---

[9] Karl Marx, *Economic and Philosophic Manuscripts of 1844* (Moscow: Foreign Languages Publishing House, n.d.), p. 99.

[10] *Ibid.*, p. 100.

It should be added, of course, that although in the Soviet Union everyone is juridically equal in respect of state property, some are "more equal than others." This means that Russia represents the future—but as yet underdeveloped, permeated by conflict, and unsure of itself. It has its own false consciousness, because instead of seeing the activity of each of its members as its own self-sustaining basis, it sees the state as the incarnation and guardian of the socialized economy.

This state, unlike the proletarian dictatorship exercised by the armed working class envisaged by Marx, is seen as an external constraint, and the individual is subjugated to a hypostatized universality that nominally includes him but is a mere ideological covering of the exercise of the interests of the new ruling group. Marx had already criticized this ideology in advance when he wrote:

"What is to be avoided above all is the reestablishing of 'society' as an abstraction vis-à-vis the individual. The individual *is the social being.*" [11]

This ideology includes the usual tired equations: the workers = the party = the leadership. People believed this to some extent, especially in the early stages, but now it is known to be a hypocritical fig leaf, and there exists in popular consciousness a definite them/us dichotomy (alienation) even though this may not be understood by a theory that transcends the given categories.

So far we have concentrated on capital and commodity fetishism as forms of alienation. However, these are only specific ways in which man may become alienated from his own activity. In a more general sense, any social system that fails to constitute itself as the free, creative expression of its members must to some degree be one of estrangement.

After noting the subordination of the worker to his product, Marx goes on to deal with the alienation of the worker from labor itself.

> How would the worker come to face the product of his activity as a stranger, were it not that in the very act of production he was estranging himself from himself? The product is

---

[11] *Ibid.*, p. 104.

tion" thesis *would* seem to run the reel of reformism backwards.

But is this a conclusive argument? What are the considerations that lead revolutionaries to reject the reformist strategy? Do these considerations apply with equal force to the reverse movement?

To put it plainly: we reject reformism because no ruling class can be expected to give up without a fight; because the institutions mediating the hegemony of the ruling class are not neutral ground, especially the state machine; and because the general ideological, political, and economic hegemony of the ruling class can only be overthrown by basing the movement on its own social forces, organizations, and institutional forms. History has confirmed, over and over again, this analysis of the impossibility of reformism. In every case reformists end up defending capitalism against the attacks of the working class (e.g., the Communist Party of France in 1968), or in extreme cases go over to the other side and lead the capitalist class in its attacks on the workers' positions (as the Wilson-Castle gang in Britain is presently doing).

It does seem plausible to argue now that the above-mentioned considerations do not carry so much weight in a case where a revolutionary overturn has only just occurred, so that the hegemony, ideological and institutional, of the new power is relatively precariously established and the mass upsurge has exhausted itself and begun its long ebb. It is not inconceivable that old ideas with much historical weight, only recently overlaid by new ones, can rapidly reestablish themselves; that deserters from the former ruling class will cross the lines again; and that the recently defeated classes, with their cultural and other resources, will recuperate quickly, lift their heads, and, finding the revolutionary body politic exhausted and disheartened, begin to take the opportunities open to them, even capturing strong points in the revolutionary institutions themselves. It is often said that there are some situations of social crisis in which the oppressed masses and their leaders have power in their hands if they only had the confidence to grasp it. May it not be conceivable that, even after ostensibly grasping power, the magnitude of the task appears so great; the resources, moral and material, so scarce; that confidence falters, and the masses and their leaders lose their nerve? The rapidly recuperating oppressors become bolder, then perhaps push forward, reestablish their hegemony, wisely integrating into it the numerous cadres, demoralized and place-hunting, willing to come over?

It does not seem to me that such a picture can be ruled out a priori. However, I do not think it gives the key to what happened in the post-October developments. True, the exhaustion did produce a social and political vacuum; but it does not seem to have been filled by the former capitalist or feudal elements, although, if allowed to proceed unchecked, the New Economic Policy may have led to it. The negation of the revolution was not one that returned affairs to the status quo ante, but one that was brought forth by—was internal to—the revolution itself. Just as in developing its power and strength the bourgeoisie produced its own gravediggers, the revolutionary proletariat, so the proletariat produced its own butchers who would strangle the revolution and build a society in their image rather than the proletariat's. However, because this negation developed within the movement itself, on the basis of new conditions and structures, it could not simply be a reinstallation of the former regime.

Once again a movement, in the name of humanity, has negated conditions that were the negation of humanity. But, once again, instead of this negation growing over into the self-sustaining positive,* free of contradiction, it has developed its own contradictions and established a new negation of humanity in the form of the repressive bureaucratic machine. But that this system, permeated as it may be by contradiction, is *different* from capitalism can only be denied by those who have no dialectical sense and simply lump together all conditions that are formally opposed to truly human ones, as indifferently hostile, thus in

---

* "... atheism is a *negation of God* and postulates the *existence of man* through this negation; but socialism as socialism no longer stands in need of such a mediation. ... Socialism is man's *positive self-consciousness,* no longer mediated through the annulment of religion, just as real life is man's positive reality, no longer mediated through the annulment of private property, through *communism.* Communism is the position as the negation of the negation . . . the necessary pattern and the dynamic principle of the immediate future, but communism as such is not the goal of human development . . ." (Marx, *Economic and Philosophic Manuscripts of 1844* [Moscow: Foreign Languages Publishing House, n.d.], p. 114)

ke the destruction of feudalism: this was accom-
the leadership of the bourgeoisie—itself an oppres-
the serfs who were directly exploited by the lords.
true that the nobility seemed to concentrate in itself
society and that the bourgeoisie was restricted in
t by the nobility and had various complaints about
Thus the revolt against feudal arbitrariness was
der the banner of a universal emancipation rather
ised bourgeois interests. Nevertheless, it is obvious
lying reality was the displacement of one oppres-
nother, *already* existing one. The bourgeoisie had
evelop its own mode of production up to a point
economic basis, to develop its own class power
tical and, above all, ideological) *before* taking on
der in a more or less sharp period of confronta-
geoisie in fact were the social owners of new produc-
tead of a simple contradiction of *forces* of produc-
ns of production, we have a complex introduction,
ing *mode* of production (i.e., both forces and rela-
bordinate *mode* of production (i.e., both forces and
ering strength, like a worm in an apple.
of proletarian revolution is strikingly different. If
gous, one could project a gradual increase in the
ooperatives in the economy, etc.; but although Marx
s the cooperatives as evidence that capitalists are
is well known that he does not base his perspective

the bourgeoisie strove for power—with tangible
heir hands of their own capacities, power, and
iority over the traditional mode of production—the
st challenge the existing mode of production from
, more or less, from nothing to everything. Indeed,
because they have "nothing to lose" i.e., no existing
Marx is confident that they must institute a class-
thout exploitation.
and mill gives you the feudal lord, and the steam
strial capitalist," what new productive force does
control and base its thrust for power on? At first
of the location of the proletariat in the existing

effect eliminating history as a form of knowledge and going back
to utopianism.

A difficult problem now faces us of locating the new contradictions in the hierarchy of the dialectic. Is the contradiction
between the bureaucratic stratum and the workers on the same
level as that between capitalists and proletarians? Or is it a subordinate contradiction, soon to disappear as part of a general
working out of the proletarian revolution?

But before we go into this, I must expand on my thesis that
the degeneration cannot be simply dismissed as capitalist restoration. What the ultraleft critics simply refuse to recognize is the
origin of authoritarian strata in the workers' own organizations;
they simply spirit in a state capitalist class from nowhere, without
explaining its origins. It is useless to point to the old czarist officers
—the working class can and did provide plenty of its own
bureaucrats. It is not accidental that the same ultralefts, who
consider the Soviet bureaucrats a state capitalist class, generally
see in the trade union bureaucrats in the West nothing but
capitalist lackeys, without pinpointing their specific role in the
fact that they also have to depend on a working-class basis.
Conceiving of the proletariat in an essentially idealist way, as the
bearers of simon-pure socialist values, they persistently avoid
the problem of bureaucratization that must be understood as a
problem *internal* to the workers' movement.

It was relatively easy to avoid the problem in the analysis of
the prerevolutionary period by seeing bureaucratic formations,
even including the labor bureaucracy, simply as servants of
capital. Thus, denying that any authentic problem exists here in its
own right, this crude approach in the case of Russia results either
in denying there is a problem (i.e., an idealist whitewashing of
the bureaucracy) or in saying that since bureaucracy was an
epiphenomenon of capital before, it must be so now—ergo capitalism still exists! Even formal logicians should be able to spot
the error here.

Although the taking of state power enormously facilitates
the opportunities for bureaucracy, the germ of this development
can easily be seen in existing proletarian organizations. The most
well-documented study of this that has appeared is Robert Michels'
Political Parties, written before World War I and based mainly

on a study of Continental social democratic parties, which provided the empirical basis for his well-known "iron law of oligarchy."

Michels argues that, in trying to overthrow authoritarian structures, the masses are forced to organize themselves and hence to produce a bureaucracy that very soon takes advantage of its position to pass beyond the control of the rank and file and develop conservative interests.

> Inspired with a foolish self-satisfaction, the ex-worker is apt to take pleasure in his new environment, and he tends to become indifferent and even hostile to all progressive aspirations in the democratic sense. He accommodates himself to the existing order, and ultimately, weary of the struggle, becomes even reconciled to that order. What interest for them now has the dogma of social revolution? Their own social revolution has already been effected. At bottom, all the thoughts of these leaders are concentrated upon the single hope that there shall long continue to exist the proletariat to choose them as its delegates and to provide them with a livelihood.[20]

Furthermore, in order to answer those who assert that the turn toward conservatism in proletarian parties is due to their becoming infected by petit-bourgeois recruits, Michels devotes space to proving conclusively that the most conservative and reactionary bureaucrats were of proletarian origin. He sums up his position as follows:

"It is organization which gives birth to the dominion of the elected over the electors, of the mandatories over the mandators, of the delegates over the delegators. Who says organization says oligarchy." [21]

Michels does not clearly distinguish among three different theses even though he asserts them all: (a) the bureaucracy developed in workers' organizations becomes conservative and joins the existing establishment; (b) the workers displace the existing establishment, but in doing so adapt themselves to existing structures so that a change of personnel is effected but the structures remain; and (c) the workers' organizations break up

---

[20] Robert Michels, *Political Parties,* p. 305.
[21] *Ibid.,* p. 401.

existing structures, but
another form of oligard

He does not clear
counts himself a histori
very crude, more or less
democracy. Thus, his fir
history:

> The democrati
> waves. They break
> newed. This endurin
> depressing. When d
> development, they
> the aristocratic spiri
> forms, against which
> new accusers arise
> glorious combats an
> the old dominant cl
> turn attacked by fr
> democracy. It is prob
> out end.[22]

In a direct referenc
of classless society (we s

Returning to the
bureaucracy, let us not
theory of revolution—na
lution differs significantl
can be obscured in such
are given in the opening

> The history of a
> class struggles.
> Freedom and sl
> guildmaster and jour
> stood in constant op
> interrupted, now hid
> ended either in a rev
> or in the common ru

What is immediatel
reconstituted under the

---

[22] *Ibid.,* p. 408.

these pairs.
plished under
sing class—no
Of course it is
all the evils o
its developme
taxation, etc.
carried out u
than of undis
that the unde
sing class by
been able to
and, on this
(financial, po
the existing c
tion. The bou
tive forces. In
tion and *rela*
in a decompo
tions), of a s
relations) gat

The case
it were analo
weight of the
sometimes cit
not needed, it
on them.

Whereas
evidence in
potential supe
proletariat m
within, and g
it is precisely
privileges, tha
less society w

If the "
mill—the ind
the proletaria
sight, becaus

mode of production, it does not seem possible that the proletariat could claim any productive forces at all, let alone new and superior ones, since by definition the capitalists own them all. However, there is one extremely important productive force that is not the capitalist's until the proletariat sells it to him—labor. The productive force that is destined to make socialism superior to capitalism is that of *a superior organization of labor*. Also, only socialism based on this is capable of taking the development of technology to its limit, so that eventually labor as such disappears and the economy rests simply on the *application of science and knowledge, socially acquired and applied*.[23]

The problem from the point of view of the proletariat is that this superior organization of labor is only *potentially* theirs. They know that everything stops when they withdraw their labor, but they do not themselves control their labor—they can only be productively active by alienating it from the capitalist. Given this, one can understand the extreme difficulty of raising to social hegemony a class, which, economically, politically, and ideologically, is almost a nullity. This is the underlying reason for the otherwise surprising phenomena noted by Lenin regarding the need to bring revolutionary leadership "from outside" the class:

> We said that *there could not yet be* social-democratic consciousness among the workers. This consciousness could only be brought to them from without. The history of all countries shows that the working class, exclusively by its own effort, is able to develop only trade union consciousness, i.e., it may itself realize the necessity for combining in unions, for fighting against the

---

[23] "To the degree that large-scale industry develops, the creation of real wealth comes to depend less on labor time and on the quantity of labor expended, and more on the power of the instruments set in motion during labor time, and whose powerful effectiveness . . . depends . . . on the general state of science and the progress of technology. . . . With this transformation, the cornerstone of production and wealth is neither the labor which man directly expends, nor the time he spends at work, but rather the appropriation of his own collective productive power, his understanding of nature, and his mastery over nature, exercised by him as a social body—in short, it is the development of the social individual. . . . As soon as labor in its direct form has ceased to be the great wellspring of wealth, labor-time . . . must cease to be its measure. . . . With that the system of production based on exchange-value collapses." K. Marx, *Grundrisse* quoted by M. Nicolaus in *New Left Review,* 48, p. 58.

employers and for striving to compel the government to pass necessary labor legislation, etc. The theory of socialism, however, grew out of the philosophical, historical and economic theories that were elaborated by the educated representatives of the propertied classes, the intellectuals. . . . Similarly, in Russia, the theoretical doctrine of social democracy arose quite independently of the spontaneous growth of the labor movement; it arose as a natural and inevitable outcome of the development of ideas among the revolutionary socialist intelligentsia.[24]

(It is necessary to distinguish carefully this point about the *origin* of Marxist theory from the question of the class composition of the vanguard party. As a matter of fact, this insight of Lenin's was not isolated. Michels quotes several writers of the 1890's on the essential role played by leaders of bourgeois origin—although he appears not to have heard of Lenin.)

At this point some may propose a much more radical revision. If the superiority of socialism over capitalism is supposed to be based on superior organization and on the ability to apply science and technology, may this not imply that the bearers of the new productive forces within capitalist society are not the proletarians at all, but the managers, technocrats, and scientists? Hence the thesis of "managerial revolution" and a new class society based on a "bureaucratic collectivist" mode of production. Variants of this thesis identify Fascism and Stalinism, consider the mode progressive only for the backward countries unable to develop in the imperialist nexus, or simply condemn it as historically retrogressive—although it is not clear on what criteria.

Certainly such a regime would be a million miles away from the appropriation of society's "collective productive power" envisaged by Marx, because *ex hypothesi* most people would be reduced to carrying out the orders of the technocrats. This means that their initiative and creativity would be wasted and their exclusion from power would actually result in gross inefficiency.

The main problem with the thesis of managerial revolution is that it has not happened. The existing managerial strata seem content to follow the program of "modernizing capitalism" and are certainly not flocking in great numbers to lead the revolu-

---

[24] V. I. Lenin, *What Is to Be Done,* in *Selected Works* (New York: International Publishers, 1943), p. 53.

tionary circles of the proletariat in a hegemonic bloc! (Of course, some of them, e.g., scientists and lower technical and office strata, have nothing to fear from anticapitalist revolution.) Equally, there is no evidence that in any of the genuine revolutions, Russian, Chinese, etc., this stratum as a whole was very much involved as a leading and independent force.

One problem in selecting this stratum as the leaders of revolution, as bearers of a new mode of production, and as a new ruling class, is that Marxism does not seem to be a very good choice to use as an ideology. One would have expected something akin to Saint-Simonism or Fabianism.

These considerations lead one to the conclusion that even the sharp social inequalities and antagonism between the bureaucracy and the workers must still be understood as the result of a process of internal differentiation going on within the institutions established by the proletariat. To establish their legitimacy, the new layers must in some way base it on the form of consciousness associated with those institutions—Marxism. Thus the ideology of the bureaucrats is parasitic on Marxism. Whereas the main area of distortion is their account of the state and the party, they cannot take this to its limit because everyone knows about the "withering away of the state." They must admit, therefore, that their own rule is exceptional and temporary. This makes them a peculiarly unconfident ruling class and heralds an entirely new epoch distinct from socialism. It also means that it is much easier for the proletariat to find its intellectual weapons in official doctrine than when it was under the ideological hegemony of the bourgeoisie. Like the structures, the ideology is a transitional one (substitution of "the" party for the class; socialism in one country, etc.), which attempts to justify the ossified deformation of the revolution. (There is plenty of scope for an extensive analysis of the relation of the ideological distortions of Marxism to the precise nature of the transitional regime.)

Is the Bureaucracy a Class?

In dealing with the question of whether or not the bureaucratic layer should be termed a class, we are in a bit of a quandary because it is not entirely clear how a class is defined. Does any group with special interests constitute a class? Or is property essential? Both Michels and Trotsky seem to think inheritance is important. Thus, Michels argues against Marx as follows:

> . . . social wealth cannot be satisfactorily administered in any other manner than by the creation of an extensive bureaucracy. In this way we are led by an inevitable logic to the flat denial of the possibility of a state without classes. The administration of an immeasurably large capital, above all when this capital is collective property, confers upon the administrator influence at least equal to that possessed by the private owner of capital. Consequently the critics in advance of the Marxist social order ask whether the instinct, which today leads the members of the possessing classes to transmit to their children the wealth which they (the parents) have amassed, will not exist also in the administration of the public wealth of the socialist state, and whether these administrators will not utilize their immense influence in order to secure for their children the succession to the offices which they themselves hold.[25]

Trotsky argues that the bureaucracy is not a class because "the individual bureaucrat cannot transmit to his heirs his rights in the exploitation of the state apparatus." [26]

Certainly, Michels' predictions seem to have been refuted by experience. In the U.S.S.R. the nepotism that undoubtedly exists has not reached the point that, on the death of an official, his heir is judged to have a right to that position. Rather, this event will tend to signal a downturn in the son's fortunes: he has now lost his protector.

However, as against Trotsky's position, it has been argued that the clerical estate formed part of the exploitive class in feudalism by virtue of its relation to the serfs on the Church lands, independently of the fact that recruitment to the hierarchy was not hereditary. The point here is that the serf is tied to the *land,* and only through this to the landowner. It is a matter of indifference to him whether the owner is a person or an institution. (Incidentally, I once read in *Reader's Digest* that Russian agriculture is state feudalist!)

Marx laid great stress on the freeing of the serfs from the land

---

[25] R. Michels, *Political Parties,* p. 383.
[26] L. Trotsky, *The Revolution Betrayed,* p. 249.

as a precondition of capitalism. It made their labor available for exploitation while also putting them under the necessity to sell it —though nominally they were free agents.

The basic problem in defining class in such a way as to include all the ruling classes in history is that the different systems under review vary enormously in the way the domination of the so-called ruling class is mediated. In this sense the concept does not appear to work as a suprahistorical static concept, but is a way of referring to a phenomenon that itself has a historical development. As productive systems change, so do the possible mechanisms of dominance. As you move from feudalism to postcapitalist societies, the more accidental the relationship between your person and your social position appears. In feudalism it is in your blood and birthplace. Membership in the nobility can hardly be separated from the individuality of its bearer. He just *is* a nobleman. Under capitalism, although we have a hierarchical society, the relationship is less rigid. "Personal freedom" exists—by which is meant the possibility of finding your own class position. To be sure, property determines this; but it is possible to gain—or to lose—property. However, the rigidities of property inheritance limit this considerably and place enormous obstacles in the way of someone born into a lower class being able to change his class.

In the case of the Soviet Union, we have a hierarchy of administrative or political function. Here the personal and the social functions have become almost completely detached. People can gain or lose positions at the stroke of a pen.

From another point of view, *capitalism* appears as the extreme term: from original community we have been splintered into atomic individuals. Postcapitalist regimes recognize the social character of production, and thus represent a partial return of man to himself. However, this occurs in a paradoxical way because, as previously noted, the social is still alienated from the individual. The institutions of the collectivity are a happy hunting ground for careerists in search of power and privilege.

The possibility of basing dominance on an all-pervasive state administration appears in previous societies only as a hidden potentiality. It could be argued that just as it was possible for the masses to do the dirty work for the bourgeoisie, so it was possible for them to do it for the bureaucracy. The emancipation of society from the common enemy, feudalism, brought out into the light of day other inequalities. It was precisely so in Russia. Hidden antagonisms became open. In previous systems, commodity markets were fringe phenomena that were apparently not basic to the social relations defined by slavery and serfdom. So previously the state functionary and his interests were seen as subordinate to other classes, based on associated modes of production (despite state organization of certain branches of production, munitions, Bismarck's railways, modern nationalizations), but suddenly the bureaucratic function is able to move in and take the center of stage when the collectivization of property destroys the power of those it formerly served. Just as the irrational feudal restrictions on labor (i.e., guilds, serfdom) and on money (usury) condemned the merchant to a marginal role, until their breakdown and the introduction of reasonable property law gave him and his capital the chance to flourish, so the manager, technocrat, or bureaucrat has to put up with the irrationalities of private property, its deadwood in the board room, its inability to be satisfactorily coordinated by the state, until, when rational planning emerges, the bureaucratic function now appears as the only center of power and the bureaucrat is unhampered by any other allegiance than to his own interest.

(Notice that I refer to the capture of power by the "bureaucratic function," not by the bureaucracy. This is meant to correspond to the point previously made that, by and large, the capitalist bureaucracy, despite certain conflicts of interest with the property owners, remains under the hegemony of the bourgeoisie. Also, there is considerable mutual recruitment from one layer to the other: managers acquire shares, wealthy men go in for politics, etc. It is not the *old* bureaucracy that takes power so much as the men exercising bureaucratic functions that emerge from the differentiation taking place in the new regime.)

Incidentally, a great play is made by the orthodox about the way in which the bureaucracy "guards" the collective property against counterrevolution. It does not necessarily follow, however, that it exercises the "dictatorship of the proletariat." After all, the bourgeois state "guarded" freedoms against the ambitions of the monarchy, but this does not mean that it represented anybody but the bourgeoisie, and it was quite possible to have another class oppressed even while they assisted Cromwell to cut off a king's head.

The truth is that the bureaucracy exercises its dictatorship in its own interest. It is conservative, and thus continually comes into collision with proletarian forces; in addition, in the main, it wishes to protect "its" state and economy against out-and-out capitalist forces.

This section has been somewhat tentative, but I owe it to the reader to attempt to state a firm position; and I shall now do this in my conclusion.

Conclusion

The root cause of the consolidation of a bureaucratic stratum in the Soviet state and economy is undoubtedly the low level of productive forces in the country. From the point of view of world revolution, this kind of intermediary formation in a particular country is not surprising when one considers its long period of isolation before the process as a whole got under way again. Nevertheless, even after the overthrow of capitalism on a world scale, the problem will still exist because it is, at bottom, internal to the nature of postrevolutionary society and its struggle to move toward abundance. Michels' "iron law of oligarchy" remains a permanent danger, one that becomes less acute as the material basis of society improves (thus allowing the masses to express more of their energy in controlling the direction of social life) and as the masses learn from experience of the danger.

The further development of the productive forces in the Soviet Union will bring the present contradictions (economic, political, cultural, etc.) to a head, and the future history of the U.S.S.R. and the establishment of socialism on a world scale will continue to develop on the basis of the working out of further contradictions.

The contradiction, as far as the sphere of production is concerned, is that between the productive force represented by the initiative of the workers and the command structure into which they are integrated and which stifles this force. The contradiction between the social forces is that between those who relate to the means of production as controllers and those who relate to it as its slaves. Associated with this are conspicuous differentials in income.

Given all this, in spite of its primitive character and its infection by bourgeois norms of distribution, consumer ideology, etc., the U.S.S.R. is a crucial step beyond capitalism and is still worth defending. Just as Marx said that the proletariat could join with the bourgeoisie in the overthrow of feudalism, but must maintain its own organization to fight its future enemies, so today capitalism is the main enemy, and we must be preparing to smash the existing bureaucracies (not least in order to fight capitalism more effectively) and fight the seeds of authoritarianism already evident in the worker's organizations.

The bureaucracy (particularly once in power in society) is a social layer developed on the basis of functional differentiations in the workers' organizations and postrevolutionary institutions; a layer that soon develops interests of its own, becoming a conservative force strangling further revolutionary development. However, precisely because of its origin in the process of proletarian revolution itself, the distinction between the proletariat and the bureaucracy is more ill-defined and variable than the sharp distinction between capitalist property owners and the proletariat. This means that the "space" between capitalism and pure socialism can be filled by an almost infinite variety of transitional forms, in the assessment of which more than one dimension must to taken into consideration: inequalities in income, distribution of power, even ideological criteria that may help to determine the direction of change, etc. I have concentrated on the U.S.S.R as an extreme case. Yugoslavia, China, and Cuba provide more complex but less severe cases, in which one should by no means assume homogeneity in the bureaucracy. There is the political bureaucracy, the technocratic bureaucracy, and even sections still in contact with the masses that might well come over if the latter engage in struggle.

Broadly speaking, these transitional regimes are ones in which proletarian power has been deformed and overlaid by bureaucratic power; in which the program of socialist revolution remains in the consciousness of the masses—albeit in a distorted way (so that the bureaucracy has to legitimate itself in these terms); and in which there exist more or less acute contradictions at all levels.

The order of the day is: overthrow the bureaucracy and establish workers' power.

The "program of political revolution" is not a rich enough concept to do justice to this (even to what Trotsky himself said). Instead, we should understand our program (and develop it) as one for a *new upsurge of proletarian revolution.* Permanent proletarian revolution must continue throughout the presocialist epoch. Its meaning will vary according to the precise nature of the fetters that need to be overcome at each time and place. There is no general formula. The demands that revolutionaries will advance depend upon what is possible and where the contradictions are manifesting themselves.

The goal, however, should always be to maximize the opportunities for the creative energy of the masses to express itself. Communism, the fullest expression of human power and freedom, is not a state of affairs to be presented on a platter; it grows throughout history through the continual overcoming of obstacles, the *struggle* of the masses. Marx has already replied to the benignity of certain rulers, or to the possibility of reform from on top:

> . . . for the production on a mass scale of this communist consciousness, and for the success of the cause itself, the alteration of men on a mass scale is necessary, an alteration which can only take place in a practical movement, a *revolution;* this revolution is necessary, therefore, not only because the ruling class cannot be overthrown in any other way, but also because the class *overthrowing* it can only in a revolution succeed in ridding itself of all the muck of ages and become fitted to found society anew.[27]

[27] K. Marx and F. Engels, *The German Ideology* (New York: International Publishers), p. 69.